Courageous Women

A Study on the Heroines of Biblical History

by Stacy Mitch

EMMAUS ROAD PUBLISHING

Steubenville, Ohio

A Division of Catholics United for the Faith

Emmaus Road Publishing
827 North Fourth Street
Steubenville, Ohio 43952

Library of Congress Control Number: 2002114044
ISBN 1-931018-09-X
ISBN 978-1-931018-09-8

Unless otherwise indicated, Scripture quotations are taken
from the Revised Standard Version, Catholic Edition (RSVCE),
© 1965, 1966 by the Division of Christian Education of the
National Council of the Churches of Christ in the
United States of America. Used by permission.

Excerpts from the English translation of the
Catechism of the Catholic Church for the United States of America
© 1994, United States Catholic Conference, Inc.
—Libreria Editrice Vaticana.
English translation of the *Catechism of the Catholic Church:
Modifications from the Editio Typica* © 1997,
United States Catholic Conference, Inc.
—Libreria Editrice Vaticana. Cited in the text as "Catechism."

Cover design and layout by
Beth Hart

Cover artwork:
Caravaggio, *Rest from the Flight into Egypt* (detail)

Nihil obstat: Rev. James M. Dunfee, S.T.L., *Censor Librorum*
Imprimatur: ✠ R. Daniel Conlon, D.D., J.C.D., Ph.D.
Bishop of Steubenville
November 18, 2002

The *nihil obstat* and *imprimatur* are official declarations
that a book or pamphlet is free of doctrinal or moral error.
No implication is contained therein that those who have
granted the *nihil obstat* and *imprimatur* agree with
the contents, opinions, or statements expressed.

To my husband, Curtis, and our children:
Elizabeth, Andrew, Joseph, and Patrick.

CONTENTS

ABBREVIATIONS

Old Testament
Gen./Genesis
Ex./Exodus
Lev./Leviticus
Num./Numbers
Deut./Deuteronomy
Josh./Joshua
Judg./Judges
Ruth/Ruth
1 Sam./1 Samuel
2 Sam./2 Samuel
1 Kings/1 Kings
2 Kings/2 Kings
1 Chron./1 Chronicles
2 Chron./2 Chronicles
Ezra/Ezra
Neh./Nehemiah
Tob./Tobit
Jud./Judith
Esther/Esther
Job/Job
Ps./Psalms
Prov./Proverbs
Eccles./Ecclesiastes
Song/Song of Solomon
Wis./Wisdom
Sir./Sirach (Ecclesiasticus)
Is./Isaiah
Jer./Jeremiah
Lam./Lamentations
Bar./Baruch

Ezek./Ezekiel
Dan./Daniel
Hos./Hosea
Joel/Joel
Amos/Amos
Obad./Obadiah
Jon./Jonah
Mic./Micah
Nahum/Nahum
Hab./Habakkuk
Zeph./Zephaniah
Hag./Haggai
Zech./Zechariah
Mal./Malachi
1 Mac./1 Maccabees
2 Mac./2 Maccabees

New Testament
Mt./Matthew
Mk./Mark
Lk./Luke
Jn./John
Acts/Acts of the Apostles
Rom./Romans
1 Cor./1 Corinthians
2 Cor./2 Corinthians
Gal./Galatians
Eph./Ephesians
Phil./Philippians
Col./Colossians

1 Thess./1 Thessalonians
2 Thess./2 Thessalonians
1 Tim./1 Timothy
2 Tim./2 Timothy
Tit./Titus
Philem./Philemon
Heb./Hebrews
Jas./James
1 Pet./1 Peter
2 Pet./2 Peter
1 Jn./1 John
2 Jn./2 John
3 Jn./3 John
Jude/Jude
Rev./Revelation (Apocalypse)

PREFACE

One of the activities I enjoy doing with my children is putting together jigsaw puzzles. We always prop up the top of the puzzle box to see the picture of the finished product, lay out the pieces, and while keeping an eye on the box lid, put each of the pieces together until we have constructed a masterpiece—that is, if you call Big Bird and Cookie Monster masterpieces.

When I first started to read Scripture, it was like trying to put together a giant jigsaw puzzle without knowing what the picture was supposed to look like when it was finished. I didn't have the box top to look at. I dipped into various passages, reading the well-known stories of Noah and the Flood, David and Goliath, Joseph sold into slavery by his brothers, and even the Gospels, yet I didn't know how the stories fit together. Frankly, reading the Bible was interesting and encouraging, but sometimes frustrating. I knew I was muddling through something majestic, but I was still unable to assemble the seemingly disjointed sections of what I knew was God's masterpiece.

Unfortunately, I know that my experience in reading the Bible was not unique. Even more unfortunate than the frustration experienced is that at this point in the game, many of us conclude that the Bible has very little to offer, and we choose to put aside the Good Book like an old pair of running sneakers, or rather, retire it to a bookshelf or coffee table to collect dust. After all, we tried, but no luck.

My own study of the Bible might have been reduced to such a fate had I not learned some important truths that helped me read the Bible with greater profit. I have written this book so that other women can discover what I did. I want to provide you with the box top to the puzzle!

No book—at least not mine—is ever written without the help of many others. I am truly grateful to the excellent staff at Emmaus Road Publishing, who work with servants' hearts, all for the glory and honor of Christ and His Church. I would like to offer many thanks to Earlene Crkvenac, Brian Germann, Kate Glass, Liz Greene, Beth Hart, Shannon Minch-Hughes, Leon Suprenant, Mary Wake, and Jeff Ziegler.

I would also like to thank my husband, Curtis, who serves as my biblical advisor and editor. His support, encouragement, and insights are a constant source of inspiration. His example of love for Christ, zeal for the truth, and tireless efforts have spurred me on to work for the Kingdom. One of his phrases of encouragement—"There is so much work to be done!"—has almost become a family motto. And so there is.

Finally, I pray that this Bible study will provide you, while learning about the story and the women of the Bible, the opportunity to reflect upon your own place in the story of salvation. The end has not yet come, and indeed, there is much work to be done.

INTRODUCTION

The Bible, which once seemed to me a collection of loosely related stories, actually fits together to tell a divine love story—an unmatched masterpiece telling the tale of God's inexhaustible love for His children. The Good Book is really our family history book, telling us how our beloved Father, throughout all of history, has sought to save the lost and unite His family forever in their heavenly home.

The Bible, while a compilation of individual books written by a host of authors in various literary genres, is even more a unified story of how God, our loving and patient Father, sought for all of history to bring home His wayward and stubborn children. The Bible is the story of our Redemption, our salvation history.

Salvation History and the Women of the Bible

We all know the saying, "Behind every great man is a great woman." This truth of human experience is a truth portrayed in the Bible, for behind every great biblical man and time period, there are great women as well. The task of this Bible study is to help you see the big picture of biblical history by allowing the starring women to guide you through the drama of salvation history.

In this study, you will be introduced to each major biblical time period and the women who helped shape salvation history. In each lesson, we will look more closely at their lives to see their virtues, vices, and struggles, and to understand how God used them to change history. In the process, we will also examine our own virtues, vices, and struggles, as well as how God wants to use us to change history.

Bible Basics

The Bible is a gift from our heavenly Father: "In order to reveal himself to men, in the condescension of his goodness God speaks to them in human words" (Catechism, no. 101). The almighty Creator of the universe, Who has no need of anything (including us), created us out of love and for love. He stoops to our level to communicate His love to us. God chose to reveal Himself and His laws to us through Sacred Scripture. We should accept this gift with great humility and honor.

The Bible is not a dead book, a classic work of antiquity, to be dissected and critiqued by skeptics and antagonists. Sacred Scripture is a gift to be unwrapped, loved, cherished, honored, protected, read, reread, memorized, and studied in the presence of God, its Author, with humility and with His assistance. When considering the Word of God, we must remember that "the Church has always venerated the Scriptures as she venerates the Lord's Body" (Catechism, no. 103).

How to Use This Study

Courageous Women has been written for women of all ages and walks of life. It can be used for personal study or small group Bible studies. I encourage you to consider a group study because God often uses the thoughts, ideas, and insights of others to change our own thoughts and convict our own hearts. A leader's guide has been included at the back of the book to help those who are using it in a small group.

At the end of each chapter is a memory verse. I have included these verses because it is very useful to be able to call to mind Scripture passages in time of need and prayer.

I hope the appendices will also be very useful. Appendix I is a timeline that provides an overview of salvation history. Appendix II is a simple chart to help us analyze vice and virtue in our lives and become objective and strategic about our spiritual growth.

The tools needed for this Bible study are a Catholic Bible, a copy of the *Catechism of the Catholic Church*, a pen, and a teachable heart.[1]

"The problem of pain" C. S. Lewis

---

[1] The Bible translation I used in writing this study is the Revised Standard Version Catholic Edition (RSVCE). It is published by Ignatius Press.

Eve
Mother of the Living

Have you ever wondered why there is so much evil in the world if God is so good? I recently inquired about the state of orphanages in modern day Russia. As a mother and a human being, I was absolutely horrified as I read a Human Rights Watch report on the conditions Russian children are forced to endure. The stories of child abuse in every form and the likelihood of a very grim future for the orphans (most will ultimately turn to prostitution, the Mafia, or suicide) are appalling. Knowing that Russia's orphans are only one of the many groups of people who endure great suffering and injustice is disturbing and sobering.

As I discussed the Russian orphans with my husband, I was reminded that atheists use occurrences such as these to attempt to disprove the existence of God. In fact, the problem of evil is the most powerful argument atheists can offer. After all, if God is all loving, why does He allow such painful atrocities in the world? Why is the world full of injustice?

More pointedly, we don't even have to look to extreme cases on the other side of the world to wonder about evil. Why do women suffer miscarriages, infertility, and even the loss of children? Why do we all seem to know someone who is a victim of incest or some other form of abuse? Why is divorce rampant and drug abuse an epidemic?

Yet, the human suffering in Russia's orphanages (as well as all other human suffering) is not a proof of God's abandonment of the world, as the deist would suggest, nor is it a proof that God does not exist, as the atheist proposes. The fact of the matter is that God has not abandoned the world. He has promised, "I will not leave you orphans" (Jn. 14:18, Douay Rheims Version), and He has kept His promise. The problem of evil starts back at the beginning of the world with the first man and woman.

Simple Story

The story of Adam and Eve and the eating of the forbidden fruit is an all-too-familiar story—so familiar that its meaning is taken as seriously as that of a childhood fable. All of us know it, much as we know the story of George Washington chopping down the cherry tree, and Jack and Jill tumbling down a hill. However, the truth conveyed in this story is much more than a mere moral lesson of human folly.

The story of the Creation and Fall of Adam and Eve tells us the fundamental truths of Who God is and of what His Creation is about. In this story, inspired by the Holy Spirit to inform God's children about their Maker and themselves, we learn about the dignity of human beings, the reason for our suffering, and the inexhaustible love our heavenly Father has for us. Furthermore, and more specifically, we learn about the equal dignity and interdependence of man and woman, the mission of man, and his rebellion against God. With this explanation, at once simple and complex, of the beginning of everything, we begin studying salvation history—the countless years in which God has sought out His children, and His children have rebelled and repented.

The Mother of All the
Physically Living and the Spiritually Dead

In this women's Bible study, we will focus on the women of salvation history, and in this chapter, that means Eve. It is difficult to underestimate the significance of Eve in salvation history. From her, we learn about who we are as women and about our place in the Creation. Because of her, we suffer, for her actions have affected all of mankind for thousands of years. To this day, we wrestle with the consequences of her behavior as we struggle with our own.

In order to understand Eve, and consequently ourselves, properly, we have to reread and study those familiar passages of Creation and bliss, Fall and misery. Therefore, before starting the study questions, refresh your memory of the whole story by reading Genesis chapters 1-3. Prepare yourself for a little soul-searching, because, unfortunately, in Eve we see too much of our own weakness portrayed.

One final note of importance on the story of Creation: In the first two chapters of Genesis, we find what are known as two separate accounts of Creation. I will refer to them as such for simplicity's sake. However, it is important to notice that these accounts appear to be two ways of expressing the same truth, but with different emphases. This is similar to what we find when we read the Gospels; each author gives us a different take, or angle, on the same events.

1. I want first to zero in on what is known as the first Creation story and the creation of man on the sixth day. Look again at Genesis 1:26-31. In verse 26, we learn that God intends to make man "in our image, after our likeness." It is interesting that the plural form of the personal pronoun is used here, hinting at the plurality of Persons in the Blessed Trinity.

a. What does it mean to be made in the image and likeness of God? For more help with this question, read Catechism, nos. 356-58.

able to know + love his creator. God willed for his own sake; unites spiritual + material worlds; dignity; freely giving of self relational; entering into communion z others

intellect, imagination, free will Memory

b. Reflect on the importance of the distinction made by God between people and the rest of visible creation. How should this distinction help to direct our moral and social priorities?

God gave man dominion over; so God has dominion over us. Vegetation, animals. Water to sustain man throughout the generations

2. Look closely at Genesis 1:27. In this first account of Creation, we read that "male and female he created them." This seems to be the abridged Creation account—no ribs, dirt, or deep sleep. However, we learn some very basic truths about human persons in this account.

a. What do you think we are to understand about who man and woman are in relation to one another and to God from this verse?

M + w equal creations of God

Complementary.

b. How should this understanding be applied in our own lives?

treat each other with respect reverence for the Creator

3. Let's now turn our attention to a part of the second Creation account. Read Genesis 2:15-25. In verse 17, we learn of God's prohibition of eating from the tree of the knowledge of good and evil. Why did God issue this command?

"you are surely doomed to die" loss of innocence; disobedience

free will

4. Genesis 2:18-23 describes the sequence of events that led to and included the creation of the first woman.

a. What is the explanation given for the creation of woman in verse 18?

not good for man to be alone, I will make a suitable partner. Relationship giving & receiving

b. What is different about the way in which woman was created from the way in which all the other creatures were made, including man? What is the significance of this difference?

woman in Genesis 2 is made of the bone of man. the same substance. Other creatures formed from what was there the earth

5. In Genesis 1:27-31 and 2:15, we learn about the duty and place of "male and female." What did God commission them to do, and what were their resources?

fertile & multiply, earth was theirs to subdue

6. The story of the Fall is like a terrible nightmare, except this one is real. Read Genesis 3:1-7. Examine the words of the serpent.

a. What is he trying to do to Eve?

tempt her to disobedience; to be like god

b. Is what he says true?

we are not gods, "we only think we are"

man - only the earth & the breath of God

c. How did Eve respond to the words of Satan, and what should have been her response?

believed his words, seduction by false thinking. NO

d. How is what the Devil says to Eve similar to what he "says" to us, and what should be our response?

confusion, falsehoods, ... NO

e. What was the temptation for Eve?

disobedience; to be like god

f. Why do you think she gave in to the temptation and ate the fruit?

she believed the "lie" that no harm would come

g. What was the fruit of her sin?

banishment; loss of innocence

7. Read the curse in Genesis 3:16 that Eve, and all generations of women thereafter, have received for her disobedience.

a. What was the curse, and how have we, as women, experienced it?

pain of child birth; desire for husband, he will be master.

b. How is the curse of the woman related to the mission of women (cf. Gen. 2:18)?

Partner, share, equal

Why did the serpent not attack the man, rather than the woman? You say he went after her because she was the weaker of the two. On the contrary. In the transgression of the commandment, she showed herself to be the stronger. . . . For she alone stood up to the serpent. She ate from the tree, but with resistance and dissent and after being dealt with perfidiously. But Adam partook of the fruit given by the woman, without even beginning to make a fight, without a word of contradiction—a perfect demonstration of consummate weakness and a cowardly soul. The woman, moreover, can be excused; she wrestled with a demon and was thrown. But Adam will not be able to find an excuse . . . he had personally received the commandment from God.[1]

The end of the story of the Fall contains many fascinating details for further meditation. First (and quite ironically) *following* their Fall and spiritual death, Adam named his wife Eve, "because she was the mother of all living" (Gen. 3:20).

Second, God's mercy is displayed fully as He expels Adam and Eve from the garden, "lest he [Adam] put forth his hand and take also of the tree of life, and eat, and live for ever" (Gen. 3:22). In addition, God places cherubim, with flaming swords, to guard the way to the tree of life. God's provisions to protect us from eating from the tree of life are merciful, for the consequences of eating it would be eternal damnation. Why? Had Adam and Eve eaten from the tree of life, we would have remained forever in the state of separation from God. He had a plan to save us from the beginning, and He did not want us to be expelled from His sanctuary forever.

---

[1] Saint Irenaeus, *Against Heresies*, bk. 1, chap. 10, in Scott Hahn, *A Father Who Keeps His Promises* (Ann Arbor, Mich.: Servant Publications, 1998), 65.

Tradition: Mary, tree of Life, bearing the fruit of life

Finally, we read that the cherubim were placed "at the east of the garden" (Gen. 3:24). It might at first seem like an insignificant detail, but often in the small details of Scripture we gain beautiful insights into the details and the depth of God's love. The Garden of Eden is considered God's primordial sanctuary, and Adam and Eve were expelled east of the garden, and out of the sanctuary, after their Fall. This movement eastward continues in the family of Adam and Eve. After Cain murders his brother Abel, he moves further eastward, further away from the sanctuary of God, to the land of Nod (cf. Gen. 4:8-16). When God's People, under the direction of God Himself, built the Temple, it was a three-part structure that faced west, beginning with the inner sanctuary, or most holy place, in which was placed the ark of the covenant. Farther east was the sanctuary or holy place, and farther east still was the vestibule or outermost court of the Temple. The Temple was designed so that as the people entered God's house they would be facing west, and when they left, they would be going east.

Physical distance is a sign of spiritual separation, so the expulsion of Adam and Eve from the garden was symbolic of their exile from their friendship and intimacy with God. Here, we begin to learn of God's pedagogy, which He still uses with us through the Church's sacraments. Even from the very beginning, God has chosen to use physical means to express spiritual realities. And in this instance, God is teaching us that sin drives us away from His presence.

The story of Adam and Eve after the garden is brief and limited to their starting a family. We do not hear anymore from Adam, but two more phrases from Eve are recorded. Let's examine them.

8. Read Genesis 4:1. What do Eve's words tell us about her understanding of children?

Produced c the help of the Lord
children a gift from God

9. In Genesis 4, we learn of the first murder—sibling rivalry at its worst. Cain killed his brother Abel because he was angry at and envious of him. The truth of the matter is that when the two made an offering to the Lord from the fruit of their labors, Abel brought what was of the utmost value and therefore a true sacrifice of gratitude to God, while Cain simply brought an offering (cf. Gen. 4:2-4). God had "no regard" for Cain's offering (Gen. 4:5), and Cain, instead of repenting and mastering sin, as God counseled, gave in to his anger and envy and killed his brother. Later, in Genesis 4:25, Eve speaks of the killing after the birth of Seth. Eve states simply and matter-of-factly that Abel died because "Cain slew him." She did not try to cover up for Cain or make excuses for him. What can we learn from Eve's handling of Cain's sin, and how should we treat the sin of our own children or others close to us?

acknowledge the truth

10. When tempted by the Devil, Eve succumbed to temptation, and a few of her weaknesses were displayed.

a. List a few of Eve's weaknesses.

b. How did she succumb to these weaknesses?

c. Write a strategy for how she could have combated her weaknesses.

_____

_____

_____

d. Develop a strategy for how we can build the virtues that will help us overcome weaknesses like hers.

_____

_____

_____

_____

_____

_____

11. Why does evil exist in the world?

_____

_____

_____

The course of history was forever changed when Adam and Eve failed to pass the test God had allowed them to endure. With the deception of Eve and the cowardice of Adam, the Devil had successfully orchestrated the Fall of the entire human race. Generations hence would be born "children of wrath" (Eph. 2:3), spiritually separated from the Father they were created to love, our only Source of everlasting peace. Thankfully, God is a merciful and forgiving Father who had a plan to get His children home—and that is what the rest of the story is about.

Memory Verse

"So God created man in his own image,
in the image of God he created him;
male and female he created them."
Genesis 1:27

9|15-18   9|22-25

Sarah, Rebekah, and Rachel

Wives of the Patriarchs

I find it strange that, I, a twenty-first century American woman, living with the modern conveniences of an industrialized country, can empathize with women who lived thousands of years ago as desert nomads. Yet, as much as things change, a few themes of the human condition stay the same: marriage, work, and children.

You see, my husband and I like to remember our five homes in the first four years of our marriage—even though those who have helped us move might not. To this day, my mother-in-law remembers how many steps it took to climb the stairway to our first apartment. And I do not so fondly remember the move with our two-week-old infant, who had just been discharged from a neonatal intensive care unit; we had a new town, new home, new job, and a new baby, and we had only been married eleven months. Soon, we would have another new job and new home, another baby, another new home, another baby, and another home. God has kept us blessedly busy!

So many of our friends and family have enjoyed the same nomadic experiences in their young adulthood and marriages. And through the drama of our modern lives, we live the ancient struggles: work, new homes, longing for children, childbirth, and the raising of children with all the joys, fears, and struggles that go along with it.

The wives of the biblical patriarchs, the great matriarchs of our salvation history, were incredible women who could probably identify with most of our struggles. In this chapter, we will examine their place and role in salvation history while attempting to emulate their example of virtue and learning to avoid their mistakes. But before we get to Sarah, Rebekah, and Rachel, we need to understand them in the overarching context of salvation history.

Refresher Course

Scripture divides the years between paradise and the patriarchs into twenty generations, ten from Adam to Noah and ten from Noah to Abraham. Within the first ten, we see an explosion of sin on the earth.

Let's start with a quick refresher: Adam and Eve were created, then fell from grace and were expelled from the Garden of Eden. They had several children, notably Cain, who killed his brother, Abel. Cain was expelled from Eden to the land of Nod and there prospered while his descendants grew even more wicked than he. Seth, another child of Adam and Eve, replaced Abel, prospered as well, and with the birth of his son Enosh, "men began to call upon the name of the LORD" (Gen. 4:26). From Seth and Cain sprang two lineages of Adam, a righteous line through Seth—those who call on the Lord—and a wicked line through Cain.

In Genesis 6, we read about how the two lines begin to intermix and how the wickedness on the earth grew to such an extent that God sent a Flood to destroy all those on the earth. Only righteous Noah and his family, along with at least one pair of every living creature, survived. After the Flood, God called the family from the ark and reminded them again of His original command to "be fruitful and multiply" (Gen. 9:7). He then established a covenant with Noah, pledging by oath never to destroy the entire earth again by a flood. He gave him, and us, the rainbow as a sign to remind us of this covenant.

Noah's Dysfunctional Family

Following the Flood, God blessed Noah and his three sons, Shem, Ham, and Japheth, and they began to fulfill their duty to work and have children. At the end of Genesis 9, there is a peculiar passage with incredible implications for the future. In Genesis 9:20-27, we read of an incident in which Noah became drunk and "lay uncovered in his tent" (Gen. 9:21). Meanwhile, Ham, his son, "saw the nakedness of his father" (Gen. 9:22). Ham went and told his brothers, who "walked backward and covered the nakedness of their father" (Gen. 9:23). When Noah woke up and "knew what his youngest son had done to him" (Gen. 9:24), he cursed Ham's youngest son, Canaan, in the strongest terms possible.

What exactly had Ham done that was so terrible? Isn't Noah overreacting a bit? After all, it sounds as if Noah were the one misbehaving! Is this just a case of a powerful patriarch taking revenge when his own misdeeds have been brought to light? It's not quite that way, and the answer lies in understanding the mysterious phrase, "saw the nakedness of his father."

Basically, this is a polite reference to sexual conduct, and in this case, misconduct. This same language is used in Leviticus 18 when God gives the Hebrews regulations concerning illicit sexual relations: "None of you shall approach any one near of kin to him to *uncover nakedness.* I am the LORD. You shall not *uncover the nakedness of your father, which is the nakedness of your mother; she is your mother,* you shall not uncover her nakedness. You shall not uncover the nakedness of your father's wife; it is your father's nakedness" (Lev. 18:6-8, emphasis added).

So what had Ham done by uncovering his father's nakedness? There are two possibilities: He committed either maternal incest or paternal sodomy. Other considerations suggest it was maternal. And if it was maternal, presumably, the birth of Canaan was the result. Take note of Genesis 9:18. Before the infamous misdeed, we read, "The sons of Noah who went forth from the ark were Shem, Ham, and Japheth. Ham was the father of Canaan." Why this special note of paternity right before the retelling of Noah's drunkenness and the ensuing scandal? After all, none of Noah's other grandchildren is mentioned before Genesis 10. It is probable that this was a case of maternal incest and Noah's wife, Ham's mother, was also the mother of Ham's child, Canaan. This would also explain why it was Canaan who received the curse and not one of Ham's other sons. And Ham could not have been cursed because he had already been blessed by the Lord (cf. Gen. 9:1).

Canaan is cursed, and he and his descendants will be the enemies of God's chosen. For a major portion of the ensuing narrative, we read about how the blessed of God (Shem's descendants) take over the land of Canaan, thus fulfilling God's promises of land (cf. Num. 34:2), which is the initial stage of His Redemption of all creation. From Noah's son Ham and grandson Canaan springs a line of wicked men—including the inhabitants of the infamous Sodom and Gomorrah. From Noah's blessed son, Shem, the partriarch Abraham is born nine generations later.

The Tower of Babel

There are a mere nine verses in chapter 11 of Genesis that speak of the Tower of Babel—a brief episode that is an integral part of salvation history. Basically, the people of the earth started to build a tower to reach heaven so that they could have the power of God and rule the whole earth. This is reminiscent of the sin in the Garden of Eden, where the original couple wanted to become like God. God responded to the builders by confusing their language and scattering them over the earth. This is the beginning of nations—God's people spread throughout the earth in need of a redeemer.

The Father of Nations

God then called a man whom He promised would be "a great nation" and a blessing to all people on earth (Gen. 12:2; cf. Gen. 12:3). This man was Abram, the tenth-generation grandson of righteous Noah. Through Abram (later renamed Abraham), God blessed all the people of the earth who, in one way or another, proclaim Abraham as their father today. Abraham was the husband of Sarai, whom God later renamed Sarah.

Abraham, as we are told repeatedly, was a man of great faith. He was called by God at the age of seventy-five to leave his home country and all that was familiar to him and go with his sixty-five year old wife to a land that God would show him. He was not told about the destination. He was promised by God that he would be made great, that he would be blessed greatly, and that others would be blessed through him. However, the little detail of where to go was conspicuously left out. Abram packed up his family, servants, and possessions and started out for this promised land of God—wherever it might be.

God established three covenants with Abraham (cf. Gen. 15, 17, 22); each broadened the blessing of Abraham and those under his influence. In Genesis 15, God promised the land; in Genesis 17, He made Abraham the father of a nation; and in Genesis 22, God promised that through Abraham all nations would be blessed. This broadening of the blessing is really God's plan to redeem His People, a plan being unfolded before Abraham, with Abraham and his descendants the instruments of blessing.

God began the plan with a married couple, Adam and Eve, and then He broadened it to include an entire family, namely Noah's. The plan broadened still further, and through Abraham, a whole nation of people, and ultimately, all of the world's nations would be blessed. How? It is through the seed of Abraham that the Redeemer would come to save not only the nation, but all of the nations (cf. Mt. 1:1-16; 28:18-20)! God would save those sent east of the garden and those scattered among the nations.

Sarah

In the following chapters of Genesis, we read the unfolding saga of the great patriarch Abraham and his wife, Sarah. She is a reputed beauty, as are all of the patriarchs' wives. (Remember that beauty in the created order is meant to point us to the beauty and perfection of its Creator.) Sarah, like the other patriarchs' wives, will be barren until the Lord opens her womb, and in Sarah's case, it is a precious miracle because of her old age.

1. Read Genesis 12:1-9. What do you think your response would have been had you been Sarai? I know mine would probably have been, "Go where? You don't know, exactly! You've got to be kidding, right?" We don't know what Sarai's emotional reaction was, but we do know that she went with her husband and endured the inevitable hardships of moving around, right by his side. How could we apply to our own lives the example of Sarai's docility and willingness to serve?

_____

_____

2. In Genesis 12:10-20, we read how Abram, out of fear, allowed Sarai to be taken into the harem of Pharaoh. History repeats itself in Genesis 20 when she is made a concubine of a man named Abimelech. Read these stories for yourself.

a. How did these arrangements benefit Abram?

spared Abram's life, received material goods & slaves

b. What happened to both Pharaoh and Abimelech?

plague; God intervened

c. What do you think this story tells us of Sarai's concern for her husband and the Lord's concern for the sacredness of marriage?

Sarai would do whatever to save her husband, she complied; Lord — intervened for the sacredness of the marriage

3. In Genesis 15, the Lord promises to give Abram a son, although both he and Sarai are quite old, and she is barren. Soon we read of Sarai's solution to the infertility problem: She would give her maid, Hagar, to Abram and, through Hagar, she would have children. Abram consents to this scheme, and lo and behold, Hagar conceives. Unfortunately, this scheme turns out to be a terrible one. Read Genesis 16.

In Genesis 16:5, Sarai is behaving like a woman scorned; she speaks irrationally to Abram and deals cruelly with Hagar. Although the plan had been hers, she was feeling its immediate, unpleasant effects on her marriage and family. However, unbeknownst to Sarai, her plan would have far-reaching effects. How has the conception of Hagar's child, at Sarai's bidding, affected salvation history? See Genesis 21:12-13. *father of the make a great nation of him (12 chieftains)*

4. When God established the second covenant with Abraham (cf. Gen. 17), he specified whom He wanted to be the mother of his son: Sarah. In fact, God told Abraham, whom he had just renamed, more things about the newly renamed Sarah. By the way, Sarai means "my princess," and Sarah means "princess." Mary is the Queen Mother of the redeemed world and, as we will read, it is providential and appropriate that Sarah, a precursor of Mary and mother of the chosen of God, would have a royal title as well. Read Genesis 17:15-16.

a. What does God promise to do for Sarah?

give her a child. to be his God - the God
of all his descendants

b. How important to the rest of salvation history is Sarah's role as the mother of Isaac? (Hint: Abraham had a child through Hagar, and Keturah, whom he married after the death of Sarah, bore him several children, too!)

Jesus is born of this line.

5. Hebrews 11 chronicles a list of heroes of the faith. Among them is Sarah. Read Hebrews 11:11. What was Sarah's heroic act of faith, and how did God bless her for it?

Mother to many through descendants
She said yes

6. Are there any areas in your life that are battlegrounds, with the bottom line being a lack of faith? Are there any promises of God, regarding the faith, the security of your family, even God's will for your family, that you lack the faith to believe? Remember, faith is a theological virtue and is given to us by grace; we need only to pray. Perhaps you could even ask Sarah to pray for you.

Rebekah

7. In Genesis 24, Abraham sends a servant to find a wife for his son from his own people. He makes the servant swear that he will refrain from taking a wife for Isaac from the Canaanite people. The servant goes and prays for a sign to let him know who will be the wife of Isaac—she will be the girl who gives both him and his camels a drink from the well. Rebekah is the girl who would offer both him and his camels a drink. Read Genesis 24:15-25.

a. How does Rebekah respond to the servant's request for a drink and lodging?

She says yes by her words + her deeds

b. According to this narrative, what are some of Rebekah's virtues? (Remember, water is heavy!)

strong, welcoming, generous of spirit
trusting unselfishness

8. Rebekah sets a standard for hospitality and service. In what ways could we practice hospitality in our own homes, neighborhoods, and parishes?

9. The story of Isaac and Rebekah is a very sweet love story. Read of their first encounter in Genesis 24:58-67.

a. What did Rebekah do when she was told that the man they were approaching was Isaac?

She covered her face with a veil; virgin
Modest; cultural practice

b. How is this behavior different from what we often see in the modern world?

_____

_____

c. How does Rebekah's behavior add to the respect that Isaac (and other men) would have for her? How would her behavior lead them to treat her?

with respect , modesty

_____

d. How does Isaac respond to Rebekah?

into his tent — married her, loved her

consolation in her @ death } his mother

10. Rebekah, like Sarah before her and Rachel after her, is barren. We are told in Genesis 25:21 that Isaac prays for his wife, and because of his prayer, Rebekah conceives. In fact, she is doubly blessed with twins! The pregnancy must have been very difficult, and as the twins wrestled in her womb, she asked the Lord, "If it is thus, why do I live?" (Gen. 25:22). How did the Lord respond to her question? (cf. Gen. 25:23).

2 nations warring (Esau + Jacob)

older shall serve the younger

11. Isaac and Rebekah's two sons were Esau and Jacob. Esau, the firstborn, sold his birthright (his inheritance) to Jacob for a pot of stew (cf. Gen. 25:29-34). Then he married two Hittite women, "and they made life bitter for Isaac and Rebekah" (Gen. 26:34). Isaac was still determined to give Esau a blessing before he died. Rebekah heard of this plan and was determined to have Jacob receive the blessing. Read Genesis 27:5-17.

a. What does Rebekah tell her son Jacob to do, and why?

to act as if he is Esau - to fulfill what the Lord had promised

b. What does Rebekah say would happen if Isaac cursed Jacob?

Let the curse fall on me. She will take the curse

c. Do you think Rebekah is being deceptive for the sake of her favored child, or is she fulfilling the promise God told her while she was pregnant with the boys?

fulfilling the promise - she would not forget (faithful to the promise)

d. What does Rebekah's willingness to accept a curse from Isaac say about her character and faith?

trusts that God has brought about this situation for her to show her trust in Him

12. Jacob does receive the blessing from his father, and Esau is furious (cf. Gen. 27:27-41). In fact, he plans to kill Jacob. Again, Rebekah seeks to save her son. Read Genesis 27:42-46 and Genesis 28:1-4.

a. What does Rebekah tell Jacob to do?

Sends him to his brother Haran until Esau's anger subsides

b. How did she orchestrate his marriage plans?

Tells Isaac that he should not marry a Hittite woman. Nothing good will come of it. Marry in her brother's community

13. List the ways in which Rebekah has influenced salvation history.

gave birth & made sure of the succession

[margin note: Patriarchal succession]

Rachel

When Jacob left his father and mother's house and headed for Laban's, he had no idea that he would find the love of his life. Jacob met Rachel at a well and quickly fell in love with her. He struck up a bargain with her father, Laban, and was to work seven years for her hand in marriage. Here is written the most romantic line in all of Scripture: "So Jacob served seven years for Rachel, and they seemed to him but a few days because of the love he had for her" (Gen. 29:20)—sigh! Jacob, however, was tricked and forced to marry Rachel's elder, less beautiful sister, Leah. He was then given Rachel as a wife with the agreement that he would work yet another seven years, which he did.

While Rachel is Jacob's favored and primary wife, the importance of Leah cannot be overlooked. The Lord, we are told, saw that Leah was "hated" and opened her womb, while Rachel remained barren.[1] Leah gave birth to six sons and a daughter, Dinah, who was the first woman in Scripture to be mentioned at her birth. One of Leah's sons was Judah, from whose lineage David and finally Jesus, would be born (cf. Mt. 1:2-3, 6, 16). Interestingly, the Son of God, Who was despised among men, chose to be born of the seed of a woman who was the less favored of Jacob's wives. We can also note that Leah is buried with Jacob in the tomb of Abraham, Sarah, Isaac, and Rebekah.

---

[1] The biblical "hated" means "loved less." This term is used in Luke 14:26, where Jesus says, "If any one comes to me and does not hate his own father and mother . . . and even his own life, he cannot be my disciple."

Finally, it is important to point out a recurring theme in Scripture: The young, the weak, and those who have no right to an inheritance, blessing, or position, often receive it by grace. Abel was blessed, not Cain; Isaac, not Ishmael; Jacob, not Esau; Rachel, not Leah; the poor fishermen of Galilee, not the Pharisees. God continues to teach His people to humble themselves and regard the blessings of life and the grace of God as gifts.

Unfortunately for Leah, it was Rachel whom Jacob loved, and she is the one considered the primary wife of Jacob. The life of Rachel was distinctive in a few important ways.

14. In Genesis 30:1-3, we read that Rachel "envied her sister" and complained to Jacob, "Give me children, or I shall die!" Jacob was angry with Rachel and replied, "Am I in the place of God, who has withheld from you the fruit of the womb?" Rachel then decided to do what Sarah had done before her. She told Jacob to take her maid so that she could have children through her.

a. How should Rachel have dealt with her barrenness?

asked God

theme: Choice   do on your own; ask God

b. Have you ever caught yourself complaining to your husband or God about the lack of something that was your heart's desire?

discern if it a good ask; then ask

c. What should be our response when we are confronted with bitter disappointments?

acknowledge the feeling; ask God
to help us accept the disappointment
patient; talk to a friend
may not be in our best interest   Romans 28:

[left margin: allow husband to express his bitter disappointment]

[right margin: example of Jesus]

15. When Jacob decides to leave the home of Laban, he consults his wives, who say, "[W]hatever God has said to you, do" (Gen. 31:16). What example is here for us to follow?

follow the will of God

look @ discernment: how do we know where our choices come from

16. When Jacob finally packs up his family and moves out of Laban's house, Rachel steals the household gods (Gen. 31:19). Laban, we are told, chases Jacob, and when they meet, Laban searches everywhere for the gods. Rachel deceives her father by sitting on them in a sack and telling him she cannot get up because "the way of women is upon me" (Gen. 31:35). In Genesis 35, Jacob buries all the foreign gods that those in his household had been carrying with them.

Why did Rachel steal the gods? Was it greed? Did she have a belief in the gods? Or did she desire to help her father's house come to know the true God by depriving them of these false ones? It is difficult to answer these questions. However, by considering this action, we can ask ourselves if we are esteeming anything in our own home too highly.

a. Do we have any "idols" that we are unwilling to let go of?

attachments (anything that doesn't allow freedom) anything to excess

b. Are we willing to cleanse our own homes of those things that will bring spiritual ruin to our own souls and the souls of those in our charge?

examen; de-clutter

17. Rachel bears Jacob two sons: Joseph, who is sold into slavery in Egypt and ultimately saves his people, and Benjamin, whose birth was the occasion of her death. Rachel is buried in Bethlehem, and the site was marked by Jacob with a pillar. Rachel becomes a symbol of Israel's agonizing wait for the

Messiah, and she is remembered in Jeremiah 31:15, a verse recalled by Saint Matthew in the context of the slaughter of the Holy Innocents (cf. Mt. 2:18).

a. What has been the biblical view of children and motherhood repeated throughout the Genesis narratives?

fulfillment of God's plan for salvation

b. How does this compare to our modern notions of children and motherhood?

not seen in this bigger picture

Memory Verse
"By faith Sarah herself
received power to conceive,
even when she was past the age,
since she considered him faithful
who had promised."
Hebrews 11:11

The Midwives, Jochebed, and Rahab

Valiant Women of the Exodus

The midwives, Jochebed, and Rahab all lived during a particularly difficult time in the history of God's People, and their valor proved them great women of history. Their lives were fraught with trial and heartache, but they triumphed over their fear and suffering to exhibit quick-witted courage in times of need—and history would not be the same because of them.

God's People in Egypt

Probably for many of us, our impressions of the Israelites in Egypt come from the movie *The Ten Commandments*: Charlton Heston, playing a dashing Moses, triumphantly leads the oppressed and suffering Israelites across the Red Sea with the Egyptians following on their heels. Of course, how in the world they got to Egypt and what they did there, other than make bricks out of mud, remains a mystery unless we peek at the biblical text; so let's take a look.

If we pick up the story of our salvation where we left off, we begin again following Rachel's death while giving birth to Benjamin. We recall that Jacob, who was renamed Israel, buried Rachel in Bethlehem and erected a pillar in her memory. Rachel's firstborn, Joseph, while the favorite of his father Jacob, was despised by his brothers. In fact, they seemed to hate him precisely because their father loved him, and Joseph's own actions fueled their hatred. (Jacob's favoring of Joseph was quite an honor since he had twelve sons: six were Leah's; two were Rachel's; two were Bilhah's, Rachel's maid; and two were Zilpah's, Leah's maid.)

While Joseph was reviled for the endearing gift of a multi-colored coat from their father, it was Joseph's dreams that put his brothers over the edge. Joseph told his dreams to the family, and their meaning was that his brothers (and in the second dream, even his father and mother) would bow down to him and he would rule over them. Joseph's brothers loathed him on account of these dreams, and even Jacob thought his beloved Joseph had gone too far. His brothers were not without a plan. They decided to sell him into slavery and make it appear to their father as if he were killed by a wild beast. They returned his multicolored coat to Israel ripped and soaked in animal's blood. Israel and his entire household mourned the (supposed) death of Joseph (cf. Gen. 37).

Ultimately, Joseph was sold to an Egyptian named Potiphar, who was the commander of Pharaoh's bodyguard. Joseph was put in charge of all of Potiphar's affairs; because God was with Joseph, Potiphar prospered because of him. Joseph was later jailed, thanks to Potiphar's wife, who claimed Joseph attempted to rape her, when in fact he refused her advances (cf. Gen. 39). (So far, this sounds like an ancient soap opera.)

Later, Joseph would be called out of jail to interpret the dreams of Pharaoh. Joseph accurately interpreted Pharaoh's dreams to mean there would be seven years of prosperity and seven years of famine. He advised Pharaoh to place overseers in charge of the land and to save one-fifth of the grain during the prosperous years so that there would be grain in the days of drought. Pharaoh then placed Joseph in charge of all of Egypt, second only to himself.

After the seven years of prosperity, there did indeed come seven years of famine. Israel, back in Canaan, heard about the grain in Egypt and told his sons to go down to Egypt to buy grain. The brothers went to Egypt, and later, after Joseph revealed his identity to them, they sent for the entire family to come to Egypt. Pharaoh, grateful and indebted to Joseph, promised to give Joseph's family the best land of Egypt and many gifts. Israel was overjoyed to hear that his son was alive, and in a vision, the Lord told Israel to go to Egypt and revealed that his descendants would return to Canaan. Israel and the entire family, with their belongings, moved to Egypt.

Israel and his family settled in the land of Goshen in Egypt, where they prospered and grew. Meanwhile, the famine was great, and in the end, all of the land became Pharaoh's and the people worked the land, giving one-fifth of the fruit to Pharaoh and keeping the rest.

When the time of Israel's death drew near, he blessed Joseph's sons as his own—giving the blessing usually reserved for the firstborn to Joseph's second-born son, Ephraim. Israel also gave each of his own sons a blessing suitable in light of the way they had lived their lives. Israel died in Egypt and was later buried in the tomb of Abraham and Sarah, Isaac and Rebekah, and Leah (ironically, not Rachel).

Later, Joseph would die in Egypt, and a king who did not know Joseph would come to power. This new ruler resented the Israelites' prosperity and subjected them to slavery and cruel treatment. The first order of business, following enslavement, was to annihilate all of the male children born to the Hebrews. And thus began the saga of the persecution of the Hebrews in Egypt and their quest for freedom.

The Midwives

1. Read Exodus 1:15-21. In this passage, we read how Pharaoh ordered the Hebrew midwives to kill all of the sons of the Hebrew women when they delivered them.

a. How and why did the midwives respond to Pharaoh's request, and what did they tell him?

_____

_____

b. How did God bless these women? What does their blessing indicate to us about the value that both the people and God placed on family life?

_____

_____

c. What pressures of secular society are you facing that contradict the Christian view of life and family in your own life and family? How does the example of the Hebrew midwives inspire you to face these challenges with courage and right action?

_____

_____

Jochebed: The Mother of Moses

2. When the midwives refused to execute the king's murderous plans, he ordered the Egyptians to throw into the Nile River all male children born to the Hebrews. In this hostile atmosphere, Moses was born to Jochebed, a daughter of the tribe of Levi (one of Jacob's sons by Leah), and Amram, who was also a descendent of Levi (Num. 26:58-59).

The Levites were designated by God to be the priestly line of Jacob, and Aaron, Moses' older brother, would be the first high priest of the Israelites. Read Hebrews 11:23.

a. What was the response of Jochebed and Amram to the king's order to kill all of the Hebrews' sons?

_____

_____

b. What do you think enabled them to respond in such a way? How does their response inspire you?

_____

_____

3. In Exodus 2:1-10, we read how Jochebed, when she could no longer hide Moses, devised a plan to try to save his life. She built him a waterproof basket out of the bulrushes (crocodile proof!) and placed the baby in the basket in the Nile at the time when the Pharaoh's daughter came to bathe. We can infer from Scripture that Jochebed also ordered Moses' sister, Miriam, to watch the child (cf. Ex. 2:3-4). Pharaoh's daughter found the baby Moses, and Miriam, who was conveniently standing close by, was sent to fetch a nursemaid from the Hebrews—Moses' own mother, Jochebed. Jochebed probably cared for him until he was about seven years old, when Pharaoh's daughter adopted him and raised him as her own. Using the chart below, list the virtuous actions and the corresponding virtues of Jochebed described in Exodus 2:1-10.

Jochebed's Virtuous Actions and Virtues

Virtuous Actions	Virtues

4. What parallels can you discern between Moses' waterproof basket and Noah's ark? Both, for example, were sealed with bitumen and pitch.

_____

_____

The Deliverer

Moses was raised in Pharaoh's home by Pharaoh's daughter. As a grown man, he killed an Egyptian who was abusing a Hebrew, and fled from Egypt fearing for his life. He spent the next forty years in the desert of Midian with his Midianite wife, Zipporah. God then called to Moses from the burning bush and directed him to go back to Egypt and lead the people out of slavery and into the Promised Land. Moses made excuses, complaining he was not eloquent, and God permitted Aaron, his brother, to go with him to speak to Pharaoh.

Moses bravely confronted Pharaoh, demanding freedom for the Hebrews. With the staff given him by God, Moses performed miracles to prove that the power of God was with him. Upon each refusal of Pharaoh to let the people go, God sent a plague, each one worse than the one before it. Finally, the tenth and final plague was decreed.

The tenth plague was the death of the firstborn. At that time, God's people celebrated the first Passover and were delivered from their bondage in Egypt (cf. Ex. 12-13). God commanded the Hebrews to begin a new calendar, and the beginning of their year takes place in what we call March or April. They were instructed to have a feast: the Passover meal. This meal consisted of a roasted lamb, unleavened bread (which symbolizes God's hurried deliverance of them from Egypt), and bitter herbs (which would remind them of their bitter days of slavery in Egypt). They were instructed to use a hyssop branch to mark both the vertical and horizontal beams of the door frame of their homes with the blood of the lamb. They were also told to eat this meal in haste, ready to move, with their sandals on their feet and with staff in hand.

The people obeyed God, and He did as He promised. All of the firstborn among the Egyptians (and even their firstborn cattle) were killed at midnight; the Egyptians' houses were not marked by the blood of the lamb. Pharaoh called to Moses and Aaron in the middle of the night and told the Hebrews to leave immediately—and they did so. They left in such haste that it is repeatedly emphasized that they had to take with them unleavened bread.

The Israelites were instructed by the Lord to celebrate the Passover feast every year as a remembrance of the day the Lord "passed over" their homes and slew the Egyptians. Jews still celebrate this most solemn feast every year, about the time we celebrate Easter.

Here, it is important for us to take a minute and look more closely at the importance of the Passover feast for the New Covenant. This first Passover meal is a type of the Sacrament of the Eucharist.[1] Jesus would later be offered for us as the unblemished lamb, and His Blood would be the mark that protects us both from a lifetime of slavery to sin and from eternal death. We have been marked as God's children with Christ's Blood, which stained both the vertical and horizontal beams of the holy Cross during the Hebrews' Passover feast. Christ tasted the bitter wine offered to Him on a hyssop branch and now offers Himself for us in the new Passover meal of unleavened bread, known to us as the Eucharist. And as the Hebrews who did not mark their homes with the blood of the lamb and did not eat the lamb were not spared, so Jesus says, "Truly, truly, I say to you, unless you eat

---

[1] A type is an Old Covenant person or event that prefigures a New Covenant person or event. An example of a type is the Passover, which prefigures the Eucharist, our paschal sacrifice.

the flesh of the Son of man and drink his blood, you have no life in you" (Jn. 6:53). We read that the people bowed their heads and worshiped when they were told of the significance of the Passover feast (Ex. 12:27). We fall on our knees in worship of the Real Presence of God in our midst.

Following the escape from Egypt, God performed miracle after miracle and provided for the needs of His people. Through Moses, God would establish a covenant with Israel, making the tribal family into a nation. He would also give the Ten Commandments to His People through Moses, along with directions for making the ark of the covenant, tabernacle, and altar. Moses would ultimately lead the people to the edge of the Promised Land.

5. Moses became the instrument God used to deliver His people from the oppression of Pharaoh. He was also the man to whom God gave the Ten Commandments and who led the people through forty years of wandering in the desert.[2]

a. Noting that Moses was saved, cared for, and taught his Hebrew heritage and faith by Jochebed, explain the impact of Jochebed on salvation history.

_____

_____

b. What is the potential impact of all mothers on history?

_____

_____

---

[2] By the way, a common misunderstanding is that the Hebrews wandered in the desert for forty years as a punishment for building the idol known as the golden calf. Actually, the wanderings were a punishment for their refusal to enter the Promised Land because they feared the inhabitants and lacked both courage and faith in God's power. In fact, they even proposed that someone be found to take them back to Egypt (cf. Num. 14:1-35).

Rahab

Following the death of Moses, the Israelites obeyed Joshua, Moses' successor. It fell upon Joshua to lead the people into the Promised Land. When the Lord spoke with Joshua, the recurrent theme of the Exodus was "be strong and very courageous" (Josh. 1:7). Joshua led the Israelites to the edge of the Promised Land, and they were about to enter the territory promised them by God. The inhabitants of Canaan, however, were not about to hand it over!

It is interesting that again, at another "hinge moment" in salvation history, God will use a woman to "swing" the course of events in favor of the People of God.

As the first order of business, Joshua sent two spies to scout out the fortified city of Jericho. Here, the two spies meet Rahab, known as "a harlot" (Josh. 2:1), a Gentile woman who was instrumental in helping the Israelites begin their conquest. With her help, the Israelites were able to sack Jericho and enter the Promised Land.

6. Read Joshua 2:1-7. In this passage, we read how Rahab risked her life for the Israelite spies by hiding them on her roof and deflecting the search for them, sending the pursuers outside the city gates. How do Hebrews 11:31 and James 2:22-26 explain the virtue of Rahab's actions?

_____

_____

_____

7. Read Joshua 2:8-22 and Joshua 6:22-25.

a. What words of faith does Rahab express?

_____

_____

_____

b. How does she secure the safety of her family?

_____

_____

c. What are the virtues of Rahab?

_____

_____

8. Rahab, a Gentile and a harlot, is one of the five women listed in the genealogy of Jesus found in Matthew 1. She was the mother of Boaz by Salmon (who could have been one of the spies) and the great grandmother of King David. Like Rahab, the story of our lives is one of constant and deeper conversion.

a. How does Rahab serve as a fine example of a convert?

_____

_____

b. Why do you think that God chose to include her in the genealogy of Jesus?

_____

_____

Memory Verse

"And in the same way was not also
Rahab the harlot justified by works
when she received the messengers and
sent them out another way?
For as the body apart from the spirit is dead,
so faith apart from works is dead."
James 2:25-26

Deborah and Jael, Ruth and Hannah
Women of the Judges

Very soon after the bright and shiny season of triumph and courage, the Israelites spiral into a devastating cycle of sin, punishment, repentance, and restoration—repeated again and again, like a broken record. The Israelites can't seem to kick their idolatrous habits, and their repeated failings are reminiscent of those of a struggling addict. The circle of temptation, enslavement, rock bottom, intervention, detox, and recovery—a circle that repeats itself—is a merry-go-round of sin that the Israelites couldn't seem to get off. This period of Israelite history is the period of the Judges.

Following the triumphant capture of Jericho, the Israelites, led by Joshua, continued to conquer most of the Promised Land. But they had one big problem: They didn't obey God. God had commanded them to take over the entire region and even warned them that if they did not, the foreigners left would be a thorn in their side. So it was. They were happy with their partial prosperity and did not finish the job that God had commanded.

What ensued was a period in which the Hebrews in the Promised Land were surrounded by foreign nations with false gods and foul practices. The Israelites, the same people that built the golden calf, were like kids in a candy store who were told not to eat, or like drug addicts at a party, surrounded by the drug of their choice. By not completely driving out the Canaanites, they were forced to live in a near occasion of sin. And succumb to sin they did.

In this time of the Judges, the Israelites had seven distinct cycles in which they enslaved themselves to pagan practices and were then in turn conquered and enslaved by their foreign enemies. In their misery, they repented and begged for God's redemption, and God answered their prayers by sending *shephetim*: judges, rulers, deliverers, or saviors. These Judges led the people to conquer their enemies and be freed from their bondage. A time of peace ensued. But lo and behold, temptation would come, and they would repeat the cycle of sin, slavery, and redemption, over and over and over again.

During this redundant and frustrating time in Israel's history, we read about several pivotal women in salvation history. In fact, in this period womanhood is represented as running the gamut of the possibilities and potential for women. Deborah was a powerful and brave Judge who led the Israelites into battle—an ancient Saint Joan of Arc! Jael used her feminine powers of persuasion and hospitality to woo the most hard-hearted of men, the archenemy of Israel. In due time, she ruthlessly killed him, thus delivering Israel from Canaanite oppression. On the flip side of the battle-hardy Deborah and Jael, we read of Ruth and Hannah's courageous sacrifice of personal comfort and their significant maternal contribution to salvation history. Their loyalty and love for family will inspire us.

Prelude

1. Judges 21:25 summarizes this time in Israel's history: "every man did what was right in his own eyes." This is not only an ancient problem, but also one with which many struggle within our own time.

a. What is the problem with everyone doing what is right in his or her own eyes—also known currently as the popular practice of relativism?

threat of selfishness, lack of discernment

b. What are the consequences of such actions, and how are they manifested in popular culture?

can choose what is not of God
embrace a lie   "death of conscience" sinful behavior

Deborah and Jael:
Instruments of Israel's Deliverance

During the time in which Deborah was a Judge, the Israelites were enslaved to Jabin, the king of Canaan. Read the story of Deborah and Jael in Judges 4:4-23.

2. Deborah summons Barak, commander of the Israelite's military, to fight the cruel Sisera, strongman of King Jabin's ruthless military operation. Remarkably, Barak says he will go only if Deborah goes with him. Read Judges 4:9-22.

a. How does Deborah respond to Barak's request?

She will go, cautions Barak that he will not given the glory of the expedition a woman will

b. In light of verses 17-22, how does this statement prove prophetic?

Sisera comes to the tent of Jael and she kills him while he is sleeping

held in high esteem, prophetess, judge

3. Deborah says, "Up! For this is the day in which the LORD has given Sisera into your hand. Does not the LORD go out before you?" (Judg. 4:14).

a. According to this verse, what kind of woman do you think Deborah was?

leader, full of faith, charismatic
strength, authority

b. Which of her virtues do you think are worthy of emulation, and in what context would such virtues be practiced?

faithful, courage
gifts of the holy spirit → understanding etc.

4. In verse 21, we read how Jael killed Sisera by driving a tent peg through his skull. Pretty gruesome stuff! Her actions, however, freed Israel from its bondage to Canaan. Like many of the women we have read about, Jael is a type of Mary. Read Judges 5:24-27, Luke 1:42, and Genesis 3:15. In light of these passages, in what ways does Jael foreshadow Mary?

blessed woman, enmity btwn you & woman
strike @ your head while you strike @ his heel

↞ foreshadowing

Ruth: The Faithful Gentile

Ruth was such a remarkable woman that she has an entire book of the Bible, aptly entitled the Book of Ruth, dedicated to her story. The book is only three pages long, and so I encourage you to read all of it. The story centers around Ruth, a Moabite (Gentile), who marries a man from Bethlehem.

The story goes that a Hebrew husband and wife, Elimelech and Naomi, and their two sons went to the country of Moab during a great famine in Israel. Elimelech soon died, and the two sons married Moabite women, namely Orpah and Ruth.

After about ten years, these men died, leaving Naomi, Orpah, and Ruth. Naomi decided to return to her people in Judah but encouraged her daughters-in-law to return to their own families. Finally, Orpah agreed, but Ruth would not leave her dear, elderly, widowed mother-in-law. She returned with Naomi to Judah and worked as a gleaner in the field of one of Naomi's relatives, Boaz (the son of Rahab). Ultimately, Boaz and Ruth would marry, and Ruth would give birth to Obed. Obed was the father of Jesse, who was the father of David, who became king. We read of Ruth in the genealogy of Jesus recorded in Saint Matthew's Gospel.

loyalty

5. Read Ruth 1:8-18 and 2:8-12. What kind of woman was Ruth?

faithful, courageous, steadfast, loyal

6. One of the virtues discussed by Boaz was Ruth's willingness to leave her family and friends and come to a strange land out of her love and devotion for Naomi. Jesus has called us to be willing to do the same out of our love and devotion to Him. Are you detached from the things of this world and attached to Jesus, so that you, like Ruth, would be willing and able to make life's tough choices?

in some cases yes - workin progress

7. Ruth, a Gentile and a woman, has been listed in the genealogy of Jesus. She was included in this genealogy as David's great grandmother, and yet not every important mother was included in Jesus' genealogy. Why do you think Ruth, in particular, is listed?

because she left her "past" out of love to follow Naomi

faith based decision making - discernment

Hannah:
Woman of Prayer and of Her Word

At the end of the period of the Judges lived a barren woman named Hannah. In fact, because of her prayers, her respect for life as a gift from God, and her willingness to sacrifice, God would use her son to usher in the next period of history.

8. Read 1 Samuel 1:10-18. When Hannah prayed for a son, she promised God that she would give this child back to God. This meant that when he was weaned, she would give him to the Temple priest, and the child would serve in the Temple of the Lord. What is the desire of Hannah's heart?

to have a son whom she would give to the Lord

9. God gave Hannah a son, whom she named Samuel, and when she had weaned him, she gave the child back to God. Read 1 Samuel 1:26-2:11. From these passages that contain both an account of her actions and her prayer, we learn a lot about the heart of Hannah. What did Hannah believe? What does she inspire you to do?

That everything came from the Lord; gave her son to be raised by Him

Samuel = child of God (margin note)

10. Hannah's son, Samuel, was the final Judge of Israel with whom God communicated directly. Samuel interceded for Israel, and God called him to anoint both King Saul (the first king of Israel) and King David—thus ushering in a new phase of God's dealing with man. In our own time, we do not have young boys serving in the Temple, but we do have men serving at the altar of the Lord in the priesthood. How does Hannah's

Sammuel : Child of God

example instruct us in the proper view we should have if our
sons or daughters are called to religious life?

Will of God comes first

================ *Memory Verse* ================
"My heart exalts in the LORD;
my strength is exalted in the LORD.
My mouth derides my enemies,
because I rejoice in thy salvation."
1 Samuel 2:1

Abigail, Michal, and Bathsheba
Women of the Kings

When I was in eighth grade, I wanted a pair of parachute pants. Everybody had them. I still remember being in art class with a girl who had a magenta pair that I was particularly fond of. Unfortunately for me at the time, my mother was not a slave to adolescent fashion trends, and she thought they were ridiculous and overpriced. The parachute pants went on the list of things my mother refused to let me wear as a teen. Thank our good God for mothers with sense and wisdom!

We can all probably remember the pressure we felt as teens to dress the same and wear our hair the same as others did. Even as adults, we can feel the squeeze to "keep up with the Joneses." As we get older, it may no longer be our haircuts that make us feel worthy of our peers, but the cars we drive and the neighborhoods we live in. Of course, all of this is plainly ridiculous! God could not care less if we have a new car that is as nice as our neighbor's. There are simply much bigger concerns in the world than our petty problems, which are caused by our vanity and lack of obedience. In fact, our problems with vanity and obedience are what truly concern God—not the kind of car we drive.

Clamoring for a King

Well, it seems as if the Israelites were struggling with similar sorts of problems a few thousand years ago. I don't mean the Israelites were coveting one another's designer camels and three-story tents with picket fences; I mean Israel as a nation wanted the prosperity and security of other well-to-do nations.

God had set them apart from the nations, and they were different. All the nations had kings except the Israelites. Actually, they did have a king: the King of the universe. But this arrangement, they thought, was too intangible and ultimately impractical. They were tired of the Judges and started to think like teens—they wanted to be just like everybody else. They wanted an earthly king.

So this is where the story of our salvation history picks up. During the seven cycles of sin, repentance, and restoration referred to in the previous chapter, God kept providing His People with Judges who led the people to freedom. The last Judge God put in place was Samuel, Hannah's son. He was a righteous Judge, but his sons were not. The elders of Israel asked Samuel to give them a king to rule over them, so that they could be like the other nations (cf. 1 Sam. 8:5). Samuel prayed and the Lord said to him, "Hearken to the voice of the people in all that they say to you; for they have not rejected you, but *they have rejected me* from being king over them. . . . Now then, hearken to their voice; only, you shall solemnly warn them, and show them the ways of the king who shall reign over them" (1 Sam. 8:7, 9, emphasis added).

Samuel did as the Lord commanded and warned them what it would be like to have a king—they would be slaves of the king and have to pay taxes. When they would cry to the Lord about their terrible king, He would not listen. Now it was the people who would not listen. They responded, "No! but we will have a king over us, that we also may be like all the nations, and that our king may govern us and go out before us and fight our battles" (1 Sam. 8:19-20).

Evidently the Hebrews had forgotten about the Lord going before them and winning their battles for them. (Did any of them remember Jericho or the conquest of the Promised Land?) In response to their words, God told Samuel to anoint a king for them. Samuel anointed a handsome and wealthy man named

Saul. And while things began swimmingly, Saul was not "a man after [God's] own heart" (1 Sam. 13:14). Then came two decisive situations in which Saul ended his family's participation in the monarchy. Both situations involved disobedience.

First, after a battle, Saul got tired of waiting for Samuel to come and make the sacrifice to God. His solution was to just do it himself. Bad choice. Essentially, Saul took on the role of the priest. His sacrilegious act was like a layperson celebrating the Mass. When Samuel finally met Saul and found out what he had done, Samuel informed him that the dynasty would end with him. Saul's son would not be king. (See 1 Samuel 13 for the complete account.)

Saul's second major act of disobedience again came after a battle. Before the battle, Saul was told to go in and destroy everything. Nothing was to remain. Saul, however, decided to spare what he thought was worthy, including the king and some perfectly good loot. Saul's explanation to Samuel for this disobedience was that they were saving the best things "to sacrifice to the LORD *your* God" (1 Sam. 15:21, emphasis added). You can almost picture Saul standing before Samuel like a deer caught in the headlights, trying to avoid Samuel's gaze and thinking to himself, "Yeah, yeah, that's what we were going to do, sure." Samuel's response was what we all need to hear again and again, trumpeted into our ears and hearts: "Has the LORD as great delight in burnt offerings and sacrifices, as in obeying the voice of the LORD? Behold, *to obey is better than sacrifice*, and to hearken than the fat of rams" (1 Sam. 15:22, emphasis added).

Samuel was trying to point out to Saul, and us, that the foundational level of our relationship with God is obedience. It hearkens us back to the beginning—the very beginning. Adam and Eve's problem was disobedience. God gave them a simple command, and they would not obey it—end of story. Saul was again trying to skip the obedience part of our relationship with God and cover up the disobedience with sacrifice, much as we bargain with God to get what we want. But God is the master of reality discipline; He always makes sure that we reap what we sow.

After this point, God rejected Saul as king of Israel and sent Samuel to anoint a new king. He sent Samuel to the house of Jesse, a man from Bethlehem, and there he anointed David, even though he was still a youth.

Meanwhile, Saul began to go mad, and David was called upon to play the lyre for him, which soothed Saul. Soon, he was promoted to Saul's armor bearer. Little did Saul know that his new and beloved employee would someday assume his throne!

David and Goliath

Soon the Philistine giant, Goliath, issued a challenge to the Israelites. He called them to send out one of their own to fight him. If the Israelite killed Goliath, the Philistines would become Israel's slaves, and if Goliath killed him, the Israelites would become the Philistines' slaves. Simple enough, except that Goliath was a giant, and no one was willing to fight him— no one, that is, but David. David told Saul that as a shepherd boy, he had killed lions and bears—and who was this Philistine anyway, to come against the army of the living God? Saul replied, "Go, and the LORD be with you!" (1 Sam. 17:37).

David went out to do battle with Goliath. He went without any armor or even a sword, just a sling and five smooth stones. Goliath mocked him when he saw him. David was not deterred and responded in words that reveal why God had chosen him to be king. David said to Goliath, "You come to me with a sword and with a spear and with a javelin; but I come to you in the name of the LORD of hosts, the God of the armies of Israel, whom you have defied. This day the LORD will deliver you into my hand . . . that all the earth may know that there is a God in Israel, and that all this assembly may know that the LORD saves not with sword and spear; for the battle is the LORD's and he will give you into our hand" (1 Sam. 17:45-47).

David killed Goliath with one stone shot from his sling. This was the beginning of David's fame. He was successful wherever Saul sent him, and soon Saul became very jealous of David's reputation and abilities. He was also growing more and more crazy.

A series of events and battles followed in which Saul chased David and attempted to kill him. During two of these episodes, David was given the opportunity to kill Saul. While he certainly had motivation (self-preservation) and the cajoling of his fellow soldiers, he honored Saul as the Lord's anointed, and he would wait until Saul's death to take his place as king. In the midst of these battles and wanderings, David met Abigail, a woman of both beauty and wisdom.

Abigail

1. The entire story of Abigail, other than a couple of one-line references, is recorded in 1 Samuel 25. Read her story. How did Nabal, Abigail's husband, offend David?

by refusing protection, food & drink to his men

2. Why did the servant tell Abigail of her husband's offense?

because Nabal had treated them unfairly, wanted to protect Nabal from danger

3. Abigail personally oversaw the preparation of the massive quantities of provisions for David and his men. Reread this account in 1 Samuel 25:18. According to this passage, what kind of woman was Abigail?

organized, efficient

4. David praises Abigail's discretion and credits her with preserving him from killing the innocent. Her quick thinking and courage saved her own people and preserved David's righteousness. In what ways can the virtue of discretion and quick thinking be helpful in our lives?

helps from making rash judgments acting rashly

Abigail's husband, Nabal, died ten days after the incident with David. David called upon Abigail to become his wife, and she did. She was with him throughout his many battles with Saul.

Finally, Saul and his sons, including David's best friend, Jonathan, were killed. Actually, Saul committed suicide by falling on his own sword when his capture by the enemy was imminent. After Saul's death there was a long war between what became known as the house of Saul and the house of David. Those who had aligned themselves with Saul were finally defeated by the house of David.

David set his sights upon returning to and ruling from Jerusalem, which would be known as the City of David. Another order of business, however, was to bring with him the ark of the covenant. The ark was a golden chest containing the Ten Commandments, Moses' staff, and a jar of manna; it was built to the specifications given by God to Moses. The ark was carried before the Israelites into battle, and when they had faith in God's power, they were never defeated. It had fallen into the hands of the Philistines, however, and David finally recovered it. It was time to bring it home.

Michal

Michal is the one ungodly woman in our study. I chose to include her because we can learn some important lessons from her mistakes. Michal was Saul's daughter and David's wife. Early in their relationship, she loved David and even risked her own life to save his. After David became king, however, she manifested some of the most despicable qualities and suffered God's worst punishment for women.

5. Read 2 Samuel 6:12-23. Michal despised David because he danced before the Lord. Michal was more concerned about how David was perceived by the people than about the worship owed to God. Michal had some serious problems with vanity.

a. In what ways do you ever withhold honor and credit due to God because of your fear of disapproval by others?

His situational

b. Do you struggle with vanity?

c. How does vanity manifest itself in your life?

d. How can you work on rooting out one particular manifestation of vanity this coming week?

e. How did God punish Michal for her irreverence?

she was barren

variety, others' perception

f. Why was barrenness an appropriate punishment for Michal?

disgrace in Hebrew people, affected her
vanity

When David brought the ark of the covenant to Jerusalem, now known as the City of David, God blessed David with victory upon victory, adding to the territory ruled by the Jews. In fact, God told David that his kingdom would be established forever. As a sign of his love for God, David wanted to build a house for the ark. Up until this point, the ark was kept beneath a tent.

God promised David that his son would build Him a house. Later, David's son Solomon did build the magnificent Temple to house the ark of the covenant.

Everything went very well for David, until he lusted after Bathsheba, the wife of a Hittite warrior named Uriah.

Bathsheba

6. Read 2 Samuel 11 and 12, the account of David and Bathsheba. Commentators are divided about Bathsheba's role in the adulterous affair. Was she a temptress or a victim? It is true that her bathing routine was a common practice of the time, and when the king called for her, she had little choice but to go. And we read she also mourned the death of her husband and her first child because of the adulterous union with David.

Bathsheba is the fourth of five women listed in the genealogy of Jesus in Saint Matthew's Gospel. The passage reads, "And David was the father of Solomon *by the wife of Uriah*" (Mt. 1:6, emphasis added). After Uriah's death, however, David took Bathsheba as a wife, and the conception of their child Solomon took place during their marriage.

a. Why do you think she is remembered as "the wife of Uriah" by Saint Matthew?

Because she is wife of David : imperfect ancestors
marriage to Uriah "righteous "

b. Why is adultery, which is explicitly forbidden by the sixth commandment, so destructive to both individuals and families? _" cheating " on spouse — "cheating on children_
trust, faithfulness, hurt, anger
breaks the bond of a covenant

c. List some practical habits that couples can practice in order to avoid this marriage destroyer.

communication

7. While Bathsheba did suffer the loss of her first child, God gave her Solomon, along with three other sons, by King David. At the end of King David's life, Solomon would reign as king, thanks to both Bathsheba and Nathan.

Read 1 Kings 1:11-31. David had many wives, so why do you think he promised Bathsheba that Solomon would be his successor?

oath he swore to Bathsheba, by the Lord

8. Like many of the holy women before her, Bathsheba kept her head and practiced courage in the midst of crisis and played a pivotal role in history. The story would have been different had there not been Bathsheba.

The Church needs women who are strong and courageous, not weak-minded and silly.

a. How has God used your serenity and courage to bring about positive change in the past?

_____

_____

b. How could you be a source of positive change in your parish?

_____

_____

9. When her son came upon the throne, Bathsheba became the queen mother, a position of power, authority, and influence.

Read 1 Kings 2:13-25. In this passage, Solomon could not grant Bathsheba's request because, unbeknownst to her, the request was essentially for his kingdom; she was not as wise as he.

a. How did King Solomon greet his mother and the idea of a request from her?

stood up & greeted her, throne to Solomon's right
for I will not refuse you

b. How does the story of Bathsheba's influence, even if her request was imperfect, enlighten your understanding of Mary, the heavenly Queen Mother, and her power as intercessor on our behalf?

intercessor, anything the King asks

_____

Memory Verse
"Has the LORD as great delight
in burnt offerings and sacrifices,
as in obeying the voice of the LORD?
Behold, to obey is better than sacrifice,
and to hearken than the fat of rams."
1 Samuel 15:22

Esther, Judith, and the Maccabean Mother
Women of the Exile and Return

Have you ever noticed that when things are seemingly hopeless, God raises up heroes? In our godless culture of death and division, God has given us Mother Teresa of Calcutta and Pope John Paul II. During the Nazi regime, we were blessed with the presence and actions of Saints Teresa Benedicta of the Cross (Edith Stein) and Maximilian Kolbe, among many others. During the rise of Protestantism, the Church blossomed with saints who led the way to holiness and faithfulness—Saint Thomas More, Saint Francis Xavier, Saint Teresa of Avila, and Saint John of the Cross, to name only a few. In American history, we look to Saint Katharine Drexel who, while giving away her vast family fortune, cared for Native and African Americans throughout the United States. France has Saint Joan of Arc to thank for rousing the country to fight against England for its sovereignty and for tipping the Hundred Years War in France's favor. The universal Church can pay homage to Saint Catherine of Siena for encouraging the pope to return to Rome from his hideout in Avignon and for her work to end the Great Schism.

All of these heroes of the faith and humanity have something in common: They stepped up to a task beyond themselves when God called, and through His power and grace they overcame their fear and fulfilled their mission. They neither shrank in cowardice from their mission, nor handed the responsibility to someone else out of false humility. The heroes of the faith unstintingly relied upon the grace of God to use them to do what was beyond them. In fact, God has quite a history of using the weak of the world to shame the wise and powerful.

In the thousand years of biblical history that followed King David, the People of God were, for the most part, in crisis. By valor and faith, courageous women saved their people and set a high mark of loyalty to God for others to strive for.

The Reign of Solomon

The glory and wisdom of King Solomon have been celebrated since his reign over Israel. Solomon was blessed by God for his humility. God appeared to Solomon in a dream and asked Solomon what He should give to him. Solomon could have asked for anything and instead replied, "Give thy servant therefore an understanding mind to govern thy people, that I may discern between good and evil; for who is able to govern this thy great people?" (1 Kings 3:9). God was pleased with Solomon's selfless request and promised him, "Behold, I give you a wise and discerning mind, so that none like you has been before you and none like you shall arise after you. I give you also what you have not asked, both riches and honor, so that no other king shall compare with you, all your days" (1 Kings 3:12-13).

As a result, Solomon was greatly blessed and to this day is renowned for all of the gifts given him by God. During Solomon's reign, he ordered the Temple to be built to house the ark. The Temple that Solomon constructed was huge and beautiful and was a symbol for Israel of both its faith and its national identity. It is fair to say that Solomon's reign is considered the heyday of Israel's power and influence. All of Old Testament history went downhill from there.

The kingdom's immensity during Solomon's reign was caused, at least in part, by his many marriages. These marriages helped Solomon to form international alliances and expand his power. However, they would also prove to be his downfall. Solomon's faithfulness to the one true God began to waver as he married women of the nations and set up idols for them. Solomon's heart went after his foreign wives and their gods, and God was angry with him (cf. 1 Kings 11). God told Solomon that because of his divided heart, He would divide his kingdom when his son reigned. God would not take the kingdom from Solomon because of His love for Solomon's father, David. Solomon reigned forty years and died.

Divided Kingdom

Solomon's son, Rehoboam, ruled Israel in his stead. Unfortunately, Rehoboam had serious defects; most importantly, he lacked the wisdom of his father. At the beginning of his reign, the people asked Rehoboam to lighten their load a bit—things had gotten tough under Solomon. Rehoboam told them to return in three days for his answer. Meanwhile, Rehoboam consulted the elders, who advised him to become a servant of the people, and he also consulted his peers, who advised him to assert his authority and increase the people's burden. After three days, Rehoboam responded to the people, led by Jeroboam, that he would increase their burdens.

In 930 B.C., during the reign of Rehoboam, the kingdom of David was torn in two. Led by Jeroboam, all the tribes except Judah and Benjamin revolted against Rehoboam. These ten tribes banded together to become the northern kingdom, or Israel. The remaining tribes were known as the southern kingdom, or Judah, and were led by Rehoboam.

In order to keep the people from returning to Jerusalem to worship, Jeroboam set up altars and two golden calves in two different cities, and even established his own feast day to replace the feasts of God. He led sacrifices to these idols. Thus, the people of the northern kingdom blasphemed and turned away from the one true God.

Jeroboam and Rehoboam were at war continually (cf. 1 Kings 14:30), and eventually they both died. They both "did evil" (2 Chron. 12:14; cf. 1 Kings 14:9), but for the sake of David, God allowed the kingdom to remain under Rehoboam and his descendants, and Rehoboam's son took his place. In the generations that followed, many of the kings were basically evil, and the two kingdoms were continually at war with each another. This was the state of affairs after Solomon: The tribal family of Israel, once united, was now divided. During this time, God began to send his prophets, who admonished the people to return to the Lord their God.

Besides continually warring against each other, Israel and Judah eventually had to face foreign invaders. The northern kingdom of Israel would be the first to fall. In 722 B.C., the Assyrians, who had already captured several cities in Israel, besieged the northern kingdom and began to deport the Israelites to Assyria. In 587 B.C., Judah fell to the Babylonians, and the people of the southern kingdom were deported to Babylon.

In 538 B.C., the king of Persia, who had conquered the Babylonians, decreed that the Jews could return to Jerusalem to rebuild the house of God. Thus, the Jews returned to Jerusalem under the rule of the Persian Empire. They reformed themselves, rededicated themselves to God, and rebuilt the Temple.

For the next twenty-five hundred years (except for a brief period of independence under the Maccabees), the Jews were ruled by other nations. There was not an independent Jewish state until 1948. Today, the State of Israel occupies a portion of the Promised Land. (Knowing a bit of this history helps us to understand the present-day conflicts a little better.)

Judith

Judith is one of a handful of women who have an entire book of the Bible named after them. This book recounts how a great Eastern army was defeated by a lowly widow.

In Judith's day, Israel was threatened by invading armies from the east. The ruthless and vicious general, Holofernes, had already subdued the surrounding peoples and soon turned his attention to Israel.

The Israelites had just returned from captivity and had recently reconsecrated the Temple after its profanation by the nations. The Israelites had heard of Holofernes's wrath upon the surrounding nations and were rightly afraid. They made material preparations for attack, such as storing food and setting up barricades, and spiritual preparations, which included much fasting and praying.

Holofernes was infuriated with them and set out to destroy them. He surrounded the hill city of Bethulia and seized its water source. He wanted to starve out the people of Bethulia, and if he captured the city, he would have free access to the rest of Judea. The fate of Israel hung upon the fate of the people of Bethulia.

They used the last of their stored water after thirty-four days and then approached their high priest, Uzziah, and begged him to surrender their city. They reasoned that it would be better to be slaves than die. This sounds a lot like the Israelites wandering in the desert after leaving Egypt, doesn't it? Uzziah bargained with the people and swore an oath that if after five days God did not deliver them, they would surrender.

1. Read Judith 8:1-8 and 8:28-29.

a. Judith was beautiful, wealthy, and most importantly, devout. What austere practices did Judith keep?

_____

_____

b. How was she treated by her neighbors, and why?

_____

_____

c. How do those around her account for her gift of wisdom, and how is her gift similar to Solomon's?

_____

_____

2. Judith called the elders before her and counseled them on how they should handle the growing desperation caused by the siege. Read Judith 8:12-27.

a. Summarize Judith's counsel to the elders.

_____

_____

b. What does she explain is the purpose of their present situation?

_____

_____

3. Judith had a plan of action, but before she would act, she prayed. Read a part of her prayer in Judith 9:7-14. How is this story of Judith and the enemy army similar to Deborah, Jael, and the Canaanites?

_____

_____

4. After her prayer, Judith took off her widow's garb and dressed herself in finery. She was very beautiful. She asked to be let out of the camp, and she and her maid proceeded to go down to Holofernes's camp. She was intercepted by a guard, who, impressed by her beauty, escorted her to the camp of Holofernes along with one hundred other men. Judith deceived Holofernes by telling him that the Israelites planned to eat what they were not allowed to and that God would deliver them into Holofernes's hand.

Read Judith 11:5-19. How is Judith's integrity shown even during her deception of Holofernes?

_____

_____

5. For three nights, Judith went out and prayed to ask the Lord to give her wisdom to know what to do. On the fourth night, Holofernes invited her to his bedchamber and planned to take advantage of her. He drank so much wine, however, that he passed out on his bed. Read Judith 13:4-10.

a. How did Judith defeat Holofernes?

_____

_____

b. Read Judith 15:9-10 and Luke 1:42. How is Judith a type of Mary?

_____

_____

When Judith showed the Israelites the head of Holofernes, they gained courage and attacked the enemy camp. The Babylonian soldiers soon found the body of their general and fled. All of the Israelites joined the people of Bethulia, and they defeated their attackers and plundered their camps.

6. Read Judith 16:21-25. Why was Israel protected from enemy attack as long as Judith lived?

_____

_____

Esther

Esther lived in captivity under the reign of the Persian Empire. Esther and her family had been taken captive by the Babylonians. After her parents died, Mordecai, Esther's uncle, adopted her, and they dwelt in exile together under the reign of Ahasuerus (or Artaxerxes), the king of Persia.

Ahasuerus held a great feast for his princes and servants, and his queen, Vashti, held a feast for the women. After Ahasuerus became drunk, he ordered Vashti to join his feast so that he could show off her beauty. Vashti refused, and Ahasuerus was furious. After consulting his princes, who reasoned that Vashti had set a bad example for the other women of the kingdom, Ahasuerus seized her crown and dismissed her from the throne. When he came to his senses, King Ahasuerus missed Vashti, so his princes proposed that they try to find a new queen. The king agreed, and they gathered all the virgins to go before the king. Whoever pleased him, he would crown queen.

Esther, who was quite beautiful and whose uncle worked in the king's court, was one of the women to be brought before the king. However, no one knew she was a Hebrew, and Mordecai ordered her not to tell. When her turn came to appear before the king, "the king loved Esther more than all the women . . . and made her queen" (Esther 2:17). He held a great feast for her, remitted the taxes of the provinces, and gave gifts.

Soon King Ahasuerus named Haman as second in power, servant only to the king. He ordered that all bow down and pay tribute to Haman, but Mordecai refused. Haman soon learned of this snub and discovered that Mordecai was a Jew. He decided to avenge Mordecai by staging an empire-wide massacre of the Jews.

Haman went to the king and asked to be given permission to exterminate this people, who had strange and different customs and were spread throughout the kingdom. He promised to give the king's treasury ten thousand talents of silver if this were done. King Ahasuerus agreed to allow Haman to do what he thought best. Haman prepared a letter in the name of the king to be sent to all the provinces declaring the destruction of the Jews on the thirteenth of Adar.

Mordecai and all the Jews, upon hearing the announcement, put on sackcloth and ashes, fasted, and prayed. Mordecai sent word to Esther of the impending tragedy.

7. Read Esther 4:6-17. Esther initially refused to appear before the king as she feared for her life—to enter the king's presence without an invitation was punishable by death. Mordecai encouraged her: "And who knows whether you have not come to the kingdom for such a time as this?" (Esther 4:14). An entire sermon could be preached (and I am sure many have been) on this sentence. Mordecai is telling Esther that perhaps this was God's plan all along and that He placed her in her present position to save His People.

Mordecai's admonition to Esther could easily be spoken to each one of us. God has made you part of the Kingdom at this point in time for a purpose. You have been put here for such a time as this, and God wants to use you! You need only to reflect upon the circumstances of your life and the gifts He has given you to discern how.

a. How does God want to use you to advance His Kingdom?

_____

_____

b. How are you living your mission, and how will you live it better in the coming week?

_____

_____

c. List one concrete action you will take.

_____

_____

8. Read Esther 14:1-3. Esther "fled to the Lord" in her time of distress and fear. For three days, she petitioned God for His blessing and grace (C: 12-13, NAB).

a. Is your response to trials and distress to flee to the Lord in prayer?

_____

_____

b. What are some practical ways that you can make prayer a larger part of your life?

_____

_____

9. Esther mustered the courage to approach the king, told him of Haman's designs, and suggested a way for the impending danger to the Jews to be abated. The king responded favorably and did all she suggested and more. Esther risked death to save her people.

a. Who or what in our culture needs to be defended?

_____

_____

b. What can you, whatever your God-given position may be, do to promote the rights of the defenseless?

_____

_____

The Maccabean Mother

After the Jews returned to Judah following their captivity in Babylon, they were ruled by the surrounding nations. The Jews were continually persecuted and enslaved by these nations. Shortly before the birth of Christ was a period known as simply the Maccabean era. This was a time in which the Jews, led by Judas Maccabeus, revolted against their oppressors. Meanwhile, the Jews were treated with particular hatred and cruelty.

The Maccabean mother (we do not know her given name) was a woman of incredible valor and sets an example for everyone, especially mothers. I love this story, and you have to read all of it to feel its full force. Read 2 Maccabees 7.

10. The Maccabean mother not only endured the sight of her sons' torturous martyrdoms but also encouraged them to suffer death! What faith, hope, and love!

a. What was the source of her faith? *all good in things from God*

God was the creator of all and to Him alone she believed. Promises to Moses

b. What did she hope in? *her resurrection, belief in the*

in the time of mercy to receive them again (to all) them   God's power + eternal reward resurrection

c. Whom did she love?

God, creator of all

+ her sons

11. When encouraging her seventh son to accept the death of a martyr rather than deny his faith, she said, "Do not fear this butcher, but prove worthy of your brothers. Accept death, so that in God's mercy I may get you back again with your brothers" (2 Mac. 7:29). This mother had an eternal perspective on life and is an example in so many ways.

a. Do you place a greater value on your and your children's eternal life than on this present life?

yes
_____

_____

b. How do you live out this conviction?

by the way I live my life ; prayer
Holy Spirit does the work
_____

12. While we are not being lined up for physical torture and martyrdom, we are being asked to forfeit or water down our values and morals. We are asked to sacrifice children for money, and our children are asked to sacrifice religious vocations for worldly riches.

a. Are you willing to encourage your children to forfeit worldly success to serve the Kingdom if they are so blessed as to be called by God?

_____

_____

b. Are you willing to exchange your earthly wealth for crowns in Heaven by raising up saints for God's Church?

_____

_____

13. The Maccabean mother and her sons were martyred because they followed a Jewish dietary restriction and refused to eat pork. While we are no longer bound to the Jewish dietary restrictions and other Levitical laws, Christ has in fact raised the bar on the moral law. Take courage: God is our loving Father and His laws, which at times seem hard, are for our good.

a. Do you love the laws of God and His Church enough to *live* by them, let alone *die* for them?

_____

_____

b. Which of the moral laws do you struggle to obey?

_____

_____

c. Whom can you ask to hold you accountable to right conduct and an increasing level of obedience to Christ's law?

_____

_____

Memory Verse
"And who knows whether
you have not come to the kingdom
for such a time as this?"
Esther 4:14

Mary Magdalene
Woman of Ministry

Finally, we reach the crossroads of the ages, when the Old Testament era draws to a close and the history of the New Testament begins. In the fullness of time, God sent His Son to seek and save the lost. The time had arrived when the "the Son of God became the Son of man: so that man, by entering into communion with the Word and thus receiving divine sonship, might become a son of God."[1]

At this most crucial crossroads in all of human history—from the beginning of time to the end—stood a woman. A young Jewish girl, the Virgin Mary, full of grace and faith, said yes to God (I've devoted the next chapter of this study to her). And with her fiat, she swung the doors to God's mercy and grace wide open for humanity. At this most important point, there stood the most unlikely of women to usher in the mercy of God.

The Son of God was born to the Blessed Virgin Mary in a cave in Bethlehem. Her husband, Saint Joseph, cared for them, and the Boy grew in wisdom and stature. Jesus of Nazareth worked as a carpenter in His foster father's workshop until He was thirty years old. Then He began His public ministry at the wedding at Cana (at the request of His Mother, Mary).

During His ministry, Jesus gathered many followers who believed that He was the One Whom God had been promising

---

[1] Saint Irenaeus, *Against Heresies*, bk. 3, chap. 19, in Catechism, no. 460.

Messianic secret
Mark 8:27-30
Mark 5: 42-43

Beatitudes

to send them. Slowly He revealed to them His real identity as the Son of God. Slowly He taught them the standards of the Kingdom of Heaven. Slowly they believed.

Jesus' ministry was strategic. He came to seek and save humanity, and He wanted His message to be spread far and wide. He called to Himself those whom He knew could be trusted with the message. From the world's perspective, the apostles did not appear to be good choices. The ragtag group of fishermen and tax collectors would probably have been a public relations expert's nightmare. Yet less than four hundred years after His death, Christianity became the official religion of the entire Roman Empire. Two thousand years later, disciples of Christ live around the globe.

One of the most important women of Jesus' ministry was Mary Magdalene. Mary Magdalene was with Jesus throughout His earthly ministry, at His Crucifixion, His burial and His grave. She was at the Resurrection and the start of the new Church. She is an extraordinarily important heroine of the faith.

1. According to Luke 8:2, Jesus had healed Mary Magdalene of seven demons. Read the context of this passage, Luke 8:1-3. How did she manifest her gratitude to Jesus?

Followed Him + provided for his (their) needs out of his resources

2. How has Christ healed you? Have you responded by following Him?

brought me from isolation into community

healed in character defects

3. In every account of the Crucifixion, we read of Mary Magdalene's presence. She defied any fear she had (unlike the apostles, except John) and braved the frenzied crowds and threatening soldiers. She looked on and endured as her beloved Jesus was mocked and tortured. She watched as the nails were driven into His hands and feet, stood at the foot of His Cross with His Mother, and watched Him die (cf. Mt. 27:55-56, Lk. 23:49; Jn. 19:25).

a. What motivated Mary Magdalene to be at the foot of the Cross?

Her love + faithfulness

b. What virtues must she have had?

Courage, strength, faith, hope, trust

c. Have you ever been called to serve or be present at important but uncomfortable times, like a hospitalization, a serious illness, or death?

yes

d. What lessons from the actions of Mary Magdalene could you apply to your own situation?

strength, courage, faith, compassion

e. How does her commitment inspire you to act?

with gentleness + compassion

4. Read John 20:1-2. Mary and the other women had prepared the spices for burial on the day of Jesus' Crucifixion. However, because of Sabbath regulations, they could not prepare His body until early Sunday morning. We read here that Mary went to the tomb "while it was still dark" (Jn. 20:1).

a. What does Mary's enthusiasm tell us about her love for Jesus?

authentic + sincere

b. Are we this anxious to meet the risen Christ in the Mass and the sacraments?

5. After Mary ran to tell the apostles that the body was gone, Peter and John ran to the tomb. They saw that the tomb was empty and then each went to his own home. However, Mary, who had followed them, remained and stood weeping outside the tomb. Read John 20:11-18.

a. How did Mary reveal her tender and deep love for Jesus?

She reached out to touch him when she recognized him. She had searched + asked until then

b. How did Jesus reward her?

He showed himself to her

c. What does this passage teach us about how Jesus rewards deep love and devotion today?

He is present. He hears us

6. At almost every major event in Jesus' ministry, women participated significantly. (One exception was the Last Supper, where Jesus instituted the Eucharist and ordained the apostles to the priesthood of the New Covenant.) At His birth, the inauguration of His ministry, the Crucifixion, the Resurrection, and the Ascension, women were present and participated in integral ways. Pope John Paul II, following the fathers of the Church, even calls Mary Magdalene "the apostle of the apostles."[2]

a. Why do you suppose God chose to include women in these ways?

Because woman was created by God ~ she is loved. We are all part of humanity

b. What is a common thread that runs through each of these events and the ways in which women participated in them?

receptive & supportive

c. In what way can you change in order to emulate more perfectly the virtues of Mary Magdalene? Choose one concrete point of action, and work on it this coming week.

listen & be open to how the Lord is leading me to surrender to him.

---

[2] Post-synodal Apostolic Exhortation on the Encounter with the Living Jesus Christ, the Way of Conversion, Communion, and Solidarity in America *Ecclesia in America* (January 22, 1999), no. 8.

Memory Verse

"But Mary stood weeping outside the tomb."
John 20:11

Mary
Mother of God and His Church

Most of the women we have studied in our brief overview of salvation history have been valiant, faithful, and loving. They have enjoyed the presence of God's grace, which enabled them to accomplish fantastic things for Him, as it enveloped significant moments and events in their lives. They were types of the woman whom God had chosen to be the Mother of His Son. The Catechism puts it this way: "Throughout the Old Covenant the mission of many holy women *prepared* for that of Mary. . . . Mary 'stands out among the poor and humble of the Lord, who confidently hope for and receive salvation from him. After a long period of waiting the times are fulfilled in her, the exalted Daughter of Sion, and the new plan of salvation is established'" (Catechism, no. 489, original emphasis, citation omitted).

In the fullness of time, God sent His Son. In the fullness of time, God chose to bless a poor girl of Nazareth, making her both the Mother of God and the Queen of Heaven and Earth.

While the women of salvation history have exemplified various virtues and performed heroic actions, it is Mary, the Mother of Jesus, who, through the fullness of God's grace, encompasses and exemplifies all virtues—both natural and supernatural—to the greatest degree. God preserved her from all stain of original sin, and she stands tall, on the fullness of God's grace, as a beacon of faith, hope, and love (cf. Catechism, no. 491). Through His grace we are made her children, and she is a faithful Mother perpetually leading us to her Son.

As the Catechism, quoting Saint Irenaeus, Epiphanius, and Saint Jerome, teaches, "'Being obedient she became the cause of salvation for herself and for the whole human race.' Hence not a few of the early Fathers gladly assert . . . : 'The knot of Eve's disobedience was untied by Mary's obedience: what the virgin Eve bound through her disbelief, Mary loosened by her faith.' Comparing her with Eve, they call Mary 'the Mother of the living' and frequently claim: 'Death through Eve, life through Mary'" (Catechism, no. 494, citations omitted).

1. Read the account of the angel Gabriel's conversation with Mary in Luke 1:26-38. The angel called Mary "full of grace," and she was "greatly troubled" at this saying (Lk. 1:28-29).

a. After Mary's initial reaction of emotional turmoil at this exalted greeting, how did she respond?

She pondered what this
could mean (discernment?)

b. How were Mary's and Zechariah's reactions to the angel Gabriel different (cf. Lk. 1:18-20)?

How shall I know this? How can this be done
he questioned; Mary accepted that
about it + then asked a question

c. How should we handle emotional turmoil?

_____

_____

2. Reread Luke 1:31-35 in light of our study of salvation history. Mary could have asked a million questions after this amazing statement by Gabriel. Why did Mary ask, "How can this be, since I have no husband?" when she was betrothed to Joseph?

Because she didn't know

Vow of virginity — ?

3. Mary responded to the call to be the Mother of God by saying, "Behold, I am the handmaid of the Lord; let it be to me according to your word" (Lk. 1:38). Again, Mary could have made excuses (as Moses did) and declared she was not up to the task, or she could have shown a lack of faith in the power of God to accomplish the seemingly impossible (as Zechariah did). Instead, she who was full of grace accepted the mission of God as the handmaid of Him Who made and sustained her.

a. According to Gabriel, what did God want Mary to do?

to have it done to her according to God's word
to be receptive, accept

b. Ponder the depth with which Mary must have exemplified the virtues of faith, hope, and love in order to accept a mission of such magnitude. Has God been calling you to a mission that requires greater faith, hope, and love? Ask God to increase these virtues in your life, and ask Mother Mary to pray for you.

4. Read Luke 1:39-45. This passage recounts the Visitation of Mary to Elizabeth.

a. What virtues does the newly pregnant Mary exemplify in her visit to her aged and pregnant cousin Elizabeth?

faithfulness, trust, hope   CHARITY
INDUSTRIOUSNESS

b. How does the prophet John respond in the womb to the presence of Mary and Jesus?

leapt for joy

5. Read the Magnificat (Lk. 1:46-55).

a. How did Mary speak of her relationship to God? *right*
praise, joy, gratitude, humility / relationship
loyly

b. Was she aware of the magnitude of His blessing to her and the world?

his mercy is from age to age
promises

6. The shepherds visited Jesus, Mary, and Joseph and told them the message they received from the angels. According to Luke 2:19, "Mary kept all these things, pondering them in her heart."

a. How is this reaction similar to her reaction in Luke 1:29 to the angel's greeting? *reflection*
She thought about it; holding it as true
(never denied or resisted)

b. What do you think is the lesson for us?

Reflect before we speak

7. As Jesus' life began with Mary, so did His public ministry. Read John 2:1-11.

a. What might Mary have been doing in order for her to know that the wine had run out?

helping with the food + drink

b. Why did Mary tell Jesus about the lack of wine?

her ministry *so that He might help the host of the wedding party (she knew he had the power to do it*

c. What did she tell the servants?

To do as he commanded

8. Mary, who nursed Jesus as a baby, taught Him to put His dirty clothes in the laundry basket as a child, and watched Him minister to thousands as an adult, stood at the foot of the Cross as He was crucified. As Simeon had prophesied, a sword did indeed pierce her soul (cf. Lk. 2:35). From the Cross, He addressed her, "Woman, behold, your son!" (Jn. 19:26). And to John, the Beloved Disciple, the only apostle at the Cross, He said, "Behold, your mother!" (Jn. 19:27). John cared for Mary from this point forward. The Church understands this to be the point at which Jesus made Mary the Mother of the children of the Church.

a. Why should we be devoted to Mary as Christ's Mother and our Mother?

Because she was His mother + he gave her to us as is mother
for her example of faith, courage, love
she intercedes for us

b. How should this devotion manifest itself?

To ask her to intercede for us

prayer, respect, honor

> Thus the Blessed Virgin advanced in her pilgrimage of faith, and faithfully persevered in her union with her Son unto the cross. There she stood, in keeping with the divine plan, enduring with her only begotten Son the intensity of his suffering, joining herself with his sacrifice in her mother's heart, and lovingly consenting to the immolation of this victim, born of her: to be given, by the same Christ Jesus dying on the cross, as a mother to his disciple, with these words: "Woman, behold your son" (Catechism, no. 964, citation omitted).

9. Read Acts 1:12-14. How did Mary spend her time in the nine days after the Ascension of Jesus to Heaven?

prayer

10. The Church teaches us that Mary was assumed into Heaven. Just like Enoch, who walked with the Lord—"and he was not, for God took him" (Gen. 5:24)—Mary did not suffer bodily corruption. Interestingly, we have tombs and relics to mark the apostles' deaths, but no grave for Mary. Why? Because there is none. Why was Mary assumed into Heaven?

Obedience, faithfulness, love, example

promise of our eternal life

11. The life of Mary exemplifies every Christian virtue and is encompassed in one of the most difficult of acts to which we are all called: service. Mary's life was entirely about serving God by caring for Jesus, caring for her family, caring for her neighbors, and caring for the infant Church. In Heaven, she still intercedes for her millions of children on earth. In Mary, we are truly taught the meaning of "to serve is to reign" (cf. Catechism, no. 786).

a. How has God called you to serve?

_____

_____

b. Have you, like Mary, accepted your mission with docility?

no _____

_____

c. To what extent do you serve with a cheerful and grateful heart? Thank God for the vocation He has given you, and make a concerted effort to be a cheerful servant during the coming week.

_____

_____

Memory Verse
"And Mary said,
'My soul magnifies the Lord,
and my spirit rejoices in
God my Savior.'"
Luke 1:46-47

APPENDIX I
The Chronology of Salvation History

THE COUPLE	THE FAMILY	THE TRIBE		THE NATION
Creation and Fall *Genesis 1-3*	Noah and the Flood *Genesis 6-9*	2000 B.C. Abraham and the Promised Land *Genesis 12, 15, 17, 22*	1850 B.C. Jacob and **Rachel** (and **Leah**) *Genesis 29*	1445 B.C. The first Passover meal *Exodus 12*
Adam and **Eve**	Tower of Babel *Genesis 11:1-9*	**Sarah** gives birth to Isaac *Genesis 21*	Jacob and his twelve sons (the tribes of Israel) *Genesis 30-49*	Moses leads the people out of Egypt (the Exodus) *Exodus 12-15*
		Isaac marries **Rebekah** *Genesis 24*	Joseph sold into slavery by his brothers *Genesis 37*	Israelites wander in the desert for forty years *Numbers 13-14*
		Rebekah secures the blessing for Jacob *Genesis 27*	Slavery in Egypt *Exodus 1:8-14*	
			Midwives save the Israelites' baby boys *Exodus 1:15-21*	
			Jochebed saves Moses *Exodus 2:1-10*	

1250–1200 B.C.
Israelites, led by Joshua, enter the Promised Land
Joshua 1-6

Rahab helps Israelite spies
Joshua 2-3

1200–1020 B.C.
The Judges

Israel is a twelve-tribe confederacy, and the judges are the rulers of Israel during this time
Judges

Deborah and **Jael** achieve a victory for Israel
Judges 4-5

Ruth
Ruth

Hannah prays for a son, and she gives birth to Samuel, who will become the last Judge of Israel
1 Samuel 1

THE KINGDOM
1020 B.C.
The Monarchy

Samuel anoints Saul king of Israel
1 Samuel 10

1000–961 B.C.
Samuel anoints David king
1 Samuel 16

David kills Goliath
1 Samuel 17

David marries **Abigail**
1 Samuel 25

David begins to reign over the kingdom of Israel and brings the ark to Jerusalem
2 Samuel 5-6

David's sin with **Bathsheba**
2 Samuel 11-12

Bathsheba secures the kingdom for her son Solomon
1 Kings 1

961–922 B.C.   David's son Solomon is anointed king of Israel
1 Kings 1

| 957 B.C. Solomon builds the Temple *1 Kings 6-7* | 930 B.C. **The Divided Kingdom** The kingdom splits • Ten tribes to the north (Israel—the people later known as Samaritans) • Two tribes in the south (Judah—thus, the people called Jews) *1 Kings 12* | 722 B.C. Israel (northern kingdom) conquered by Assyria, and the people are deported *2 Kings 17* **Judith** *Judith* | 587 B.C. Judah (southern kingdom) conquered, and the people are deported to Babylon *2 Kings 24-25* **Queen Esther** saves the Jews from extermination *Esther* | 538 B.C. Jewish remnant returns to Jerusalem from Babylon *Ezra 1* |

520–515 B.C.
Reconstruction
of the Temple
Ezra 3

333 B.C. –
4 B.C.

The final years
of the Old
Covenant

Seleucids
rule the
Jewish people
Maccabees revolt
1 Maccabees 1-2

The Maccabean
mother
2 Maccabees 7

**NEW
COVENANT**
4 B.C.
Mary gives
birth to Jesus
Luke 2

A.D. 27
The wedding
at Cana—start
of Jesus' public
ministry
John 2:1-11

A.D. 30
The Crucifixion
and Resurrection
of Jesus Christ
John 19-20

Jesus appears
to **Mary
Magdalene,**
and she tells
the apostles
John 20:11-18

Jesus ascends
into Heaven
Acts 1:9

The Holy Spirit
descends on the
apostles, and
the Church
is born
Acts 2:1-4

APPENDIX II

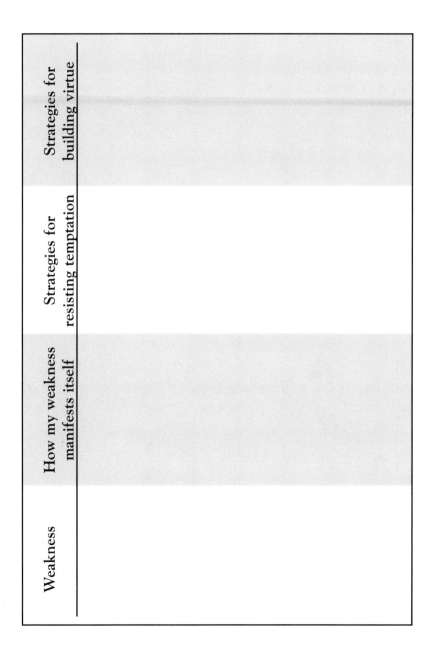

Weakness	How my weakness manifests itself	Strategies for resisting temptation	Strategies for building virtue

Strategizing for Virtue

BIBLE STUDY LEADER'S GUIDE
General Suggestions

Thank you for offering your time and energy to lead this Bible study. It is a great privilege to serve the Lord by serving others. He Who is faithful will reward your generosity. To help you get started, here are a few general suggestions for leading a small group Bible study.

1. How do you start a Bible study group? Simply ask your friends, colleagues, neighbors, and fellow parishioners if they would like to join you in a Bible study. Tell them what the study is about and when and where you would like to meet. It is helpful if you are able to meet at an agreed-upon time and place, preferably once a week in someone's home. Because this Bible study is designed to facilitate discussion, a small number of members is preferable. A group of five or six is ideal, but a few less or more would be fine.

2. You should cover approximately one chapter per week in one to two hours. However, some chapters may take more time, depending on the amount of group discussion. Feel free to allow your group to take more time on the chapters when the discussion is particularly edifying and productive. It is okay if a chapter takes more than one week to cover.

3. The atmosphere of the Bible study should be comfortable and relaxed. It is important that everyone feels respected and is able to share her thoughts. You may want to provide refreshments or have group members take turns providing a small treat.

4. Each meeting time should begin and end with prayer. It is also a good idea to have members share their personal prayer

requests and make a commitment to pray for one another throughout the week.

5. As leader, your job will be to facilitate and move along the discussion, as well as to correct any misunderstandings. You will want to prepare for the Bible study by completing the assigned chapter and thinking of extra questions you will ask. The other members should prepare for the study time by completing the assigned chapter before they arrive.

6. Spend some time each week praying for the success of the Bible study and for each of the women in your group.

Answers, Information, and More Questions

The next part of the leader's guide contains the answers to the questions asked in the lessons, as well as additional background information and questions for group discussion. The answers to the questions are marked with an "A," "I" sets off any additional information, and "Q" denotes suggested questions for discussion printed in italics. You may feel free to include or leave out any of the questions and information in your weekly study.

Lesson 1
Eve: Mother of the Living

1. A:

  a. We were created with the capacity to know and love like God. We were endowed with a mind to know God and a will to love God. These faculties were damaged but not destroyed by the Fall.

  b. In all of God's visible creation, only human persons were created in the image and likeness of God. The rest of visible creation was made for man and in subjection to him. Therefore, while we have a responsibility to be good stewards of creation and God's creatures, the care of human persons must always take pride of place. While perhaps we should concern ourselves with "saving the baby seals," such actions must take second place to "saving the baby humans."

2. A:

  a. Male and female are created equal in their dignity as creatures of God and as persons made in the image and likeness of God.

  b. Answers will vary. In light of our unique vocations, men and women should offer mutual respect to one another as creatures made in the image of God.

3. A: God issued the command as a test of Adam and Eve's obedience. If they would eat of the tree, they would suffer spiritual death, and eventually physical death and eternal separation from God.

4. A:

  a. Man needed a companion and helper.

b. Woman was created from the side of man, not from the the dust of the earth as man was. The woman comes from the man, and together the two make up humanity as created by God.

5. A: Adam and Eve were told by God to work and have a family. They had everything on the earth at their disposal.

6. A:
a. The Devil is trying to make Eve think that God has deprived her of something of great value.
b. No: Satan is a master of distorting the truth. It is true the tree would allow them to know good and evil and that they would not die an immediate physical death. However, they would die spiritually, and eventually, physically. Also, they would not be more like God, but less so.

Q: *How does Satan still tempt us, in our modern world, to think that perhaps God is depriving us of something? Does he make the moral law seem burdensome? What lies of Satan has our culture bought into?*

c. She thought over what the serpent had said, ate the fruit, and gave some to her husband. She should never have even considered the words of the Devil. God's command was simple and clear, and there was no reason even to entertain thoughts of disobedience.

I: Eve went through all three stages of sin. She was tempted, she considered committing the sin, and finally she acted.

d. The Devil continually attempts to deceive us, as he deceived Eve, by making good appear evil and evil appear good. We need to cling to the truths of God, be on our guard, and put on the armor of God (cf. Eph. 6:10-18).

e. Eve was tempted by a material good and by the deception that it would make her wise.

f. She refused to cling to the command of God, which she knew to be true. Eve gave in to pride at many levels, the most basic being that she would even question the command of God.

g. The fruit of the sin was the Fall of humanity and the curses, as well as a loss of the preternatural gifts (cf. Catechism, no. 400).

7. A:

a. We experience pain in childbearing and a ruptured, disordered relationship with the opposite sex.

b. The woman was created to be a helpmate and companion to man and to aid in fulfilling God's command to "[b]e fruitful and multiply" (Gen. 1:28). Our bodies give manifest witness to our part in the plan: childbirth and the rearing of children. The curse is related to the most crucial aspect of woman's life and calling. She will bear her children in pain, and her relationship as a helpmate has been distorted.

8. A: She believed children were from God and not entirely her own doing.

9. A: The sin of those nearest and dearest to us are the most difficult ones for us to handle appropriately because our fondness tends to blind or distort our attitudes. Like Eve, we must not take excuses or soft-pedal the gravity of sin in those we love, particularly when it is of grave matter.

Christ must serve as our model. We must seek to build and maintain the relationship, but we cannot ever condone the sin or participate in it. True love wishes for what is eternally best for those we love, not what might be temporarily comfortable.

Of particular concern here are the sins of our children. While we cannot control our children's actions, we are responsible for what we can control. We will be held accountable for the places we allow our children to go, the clothes we allow them to wear, and the movies, magazines, video games, Internet sites, and books we allow them look at. We are responsible for protecting our children from near occasions of sin and for providing wholesome environments that will allow them to grow in virtue. No easy task, I am sure—not without the grace of God, that is.

10. A:

    a. Her weaknesses include her lack of discipline, improper curiosity, selfishness, and pride.

    b. She entered into a conversation with the Devil, even when he started the conversation by contradicting God's Word. Because she saw the fruit was beautiful, she ate, seeing that the fruit was able to make her know what God knows.

    c. Eve should have removed herself from the situation. Her undisciplined curiosity could have been tamed if she had recalled to her mind the truths of God. She also could have reminded herself who she was and Who God is.

    d. 1. Fill the mind with what is true and good and beautiful.

       2. Mortify the mind and curiosity by denying yourself immediate intellectual gratification. (One strategy to mortify the mind when reading is to set a timer and stop reading, wherever you are on the page, when the timer goes off.)

       3. Grow in genuine love of God through frequent prayer, participation in the sacraments, and reading of the Gospels.

       4. Establish a regular prayer routine.

5. Establish reminders that would help you to pray in stressful situations, rather than rely on your own power.

11. A: Evil exists in the world because Adam and Eve, by their own free will, chose to eat of the tree of the knowledge of good and evil. Their act of disobedience, committed while they were in a state of perfect innocence and bliss, separated them and (through original sin) us from the relationship that originally existed between God and humanity. Their disobedience also caused a loss of the preternatural gifts. The original harmony, order, and life that previously existed in the world are now changed to disharmony, disorder, and death.

Lesson 2
Sarah, Rebekah, Rachel: Wives of the Patriarchs

Sarah

1. Allow the women an opportunity to share their ideas. Imagine the lack of peace that would have occurred in the marriage had Sarai disputed with Abram.

I: You could draw the women's attention to Ephesians 5 and discuss the headship of the husband and the meaning of submission in marriage.

2. A:
   a. Pharaoh "dealt well with Abram" (Gen. 12:16).
   b. The Lord plagued both Pharaoh and Abimelech and those under their influence.
   c. From both Sarai's and Abram's perspective, Abram would have been dead had she not protected him with this scheme. In this instance of Abram's cowardice, we can see courage on the part of Sarai to sacrifice herself for the welfare of her husband.

   Remember, Abram and Sarai did not have the sixth commandment to warn them against adultery—they had only the natural law. Adultery will always eat away at a marriage (as we see later when Abram takes a concubine named Hagar), and the marriage bed was always sacred, whether or not its sacredness was recognized by the couple. Thus, God protected Abram and Sarai's marriage from the spouses themselves in both of these instances.

3. A: God promised to establish a nation out of Ishmael, and He did. Arabs claim they are descendants of Abraham through his son Ishmael.

4. A:
   a. God promises to bless Sarah and to make her the mother of nations.
   b. Her promise is complimentary to Abraham's: If he is the father of nations, she is the mother. More importantly, the children of blessing and inheritance must trace their lineage to their mother, Sarah, to be sure they are children of the promise.

5. A: Sarah believed that God would do as He promised, and she "received power to conceive" (Heb. 11:11).

6. Allow the women to share their responses.

Rebekah
7. A:
   a. She immediately gave him the water she had been carrying and offered to get the water for his camels. She *ran* to get the water for all of his camels until they were done drinking.
   b. Rebekah was hospitable, generous, quick, hardworking, and selfless. She did not think about how heavy the water was, nor did she consider that she would have to get all the water for her own family again. Instead, she thought about the needs of the traveler.

8. Allow the women to share their own ideas. A few of my own and those that I've borrowed include inviting families over for dinner or brunch after Sunday Mass, hosting a neighborhood cookout, organizing meals for families with newborn babies or those who are sick, and visiting the new members of the parish.

9. A:

    a. She covered herself with her veil.

    b. Immodesty tends to be the way in which many women in our present culture attempt to attract men.

    c. Rebekah honored the customs of her time, did not allow herself to be gawked at, and protected Isaac from any sin that would be caused by immodesty on her part. Rebekah's actions showed that she respected both herself and Isaac.

    d. Isaac married Rebekah, "and he loved her" (Gen. 24:67).

I: This is one of the few explicit statements of emotional love in Scripture. It is interesting to note that Isaac was the only patriarch who did *not* take any concubines. When his wife was barren, he turned in prayer to the Lord, and not to concubines, to secure his legacy.

Q: *How does our dress affect those around us? What is the importance of modest dress? What type of clothing should we allow our children to wear?*

10. A: The two children in her would become divided nations, and the elder would serve the younger.

11. A:

    a. Rebekah tells Jacob to go and get her two kids so that she can prepare them for Isaac and have Jacob receive the blessing instead of Esau.

    b. She would take the curse upon herself.

    c. This is, of course, a matter of interpretation. I think that Rebekah, whose character has proven to be godly and worthy of her husband, was facilitating the plan of God.

    d. Rebekah's willingness to accept the curse revealed both her love for her son and her faith that what she was doing was right. She was willing to accept the consequences of her actions.

12. A:
   a. Rebekah tells him to go to her brother Laban's home until Esau's wrath has subsided.
   b. She influenced Isaac to instruct his son to marry one of Laban's daughters and not one of the Canaanite women.

13. A: Rebekah gave birth to the third patriarch of God and secured his succession.

Rachel
14. A:
   a. Rachel should have prayed, asked her husband to pray a Isaac had done, and waited on the Lord.
   b. Allow the women to share their thoughts.
   c. We should pray and seek constructive solutions.

15. A: Trust that God will direct our husbands, as the heads of our homes, to do what is best for our families. If our husbands say that God has told them to do something, we should be supportive so long as it is not in contradiction to what we know to be the moral law of God.

16.
   a.–b. Allow the women to share their thoughts and ideas.

17. A:
   a. Children and motherhood are a sign of God's blessing.
   b. Childbearing today is sometimes considered a disease that we must prevent with various forms of contraception. Motherhood is no longer a badge of honor, but is often seen as a mistake or the life choice of a fool.

Lesson 3
The Midwives, Jochebed, and Rahab:
Valiant Women of the Exodus

The Midwives
1. A:

a. Because the midwives feared God, they let the male children live. The midwives told Pharaoh that the Hebrew women delivered their babies before they could get to them. Pharaoh evidently believed their story.

b. "[B]ecause the midwives feared God he gave them families"(Ex. 1:21). Family life and childbearing are blessings from God.

c. Allow the women the opportunity to share their thoughts and ideas.

Jochebed: The Mother of Moses
2. A:

a. Moses' parents were not afraid of the king's edict, and theyhid their baby for three months.

b. Answers will vary. I think that Moses' parents, like the midwives, feared God more than they feared a pharaoh and were willing to act on their faith, no matter the cost.

3. A:
Jochebed's Virtuous Actions and Virtues

Virtuous Actions	Virtues
Hid her child who was sentenced to die	Courage
Built him an ark made out of material that would keep him safe from the dangers of the Nile—like crocodiles!	Prudence
Set her daughter to watch over Moses	Wisdom

4. A: The basic parallel between the ark of Noah and the ark of Moses is that both of these arks carried the remnant of a destroyed people. Each of these survivors then acted as the "redeemer" of the people. Interestingly, both were sealed with bitumen and pitch, and both traveled through rough and dangerous waters.

5. A:

a. Jochebed saved the redeemer who would save Israel. She gave birth to Moses, preserved his life, and educated him. Jochebed indirectly, through the proper and heroic care of her child, provided the means of the Hebrews' freedom from Egypt. The subsequent acts of the Hebrews, and the ultimate coming of the Messiah, are evidence of the interconnectedness of history and of all people. Our acts of courage and faith, and yes, sin, will affect current events and the world to come.

b. We do not know what God's plans are for our children, but we do know He does have a plan for them. When we raise our children according to the will of God and with His grace, we are likely giving Him a person unencumbered by habitual sin and, in fact, enabled to do great things. Who knows, maybe you have the first American pope living under your roof! Right now he may have a runny nose and dirty hands and be asking for a cookie. But someday, God may use those hands you have cleansed to offer the sacrifice of our Lord's Body and Blood, and God may inspire him to fast to save souls. It depends on our love and parenting, our children's choices, and God's grace.

Rahab

6. A: Both passages highlight the gift of faith to Rahab. This faith, in conjunction with her actions, saved her from destruction and justified her.

7. A:

   a. Rahab tells the spies that the people of Jericho have heard of God's mighty works on behalf of the Hebrews and that she believes that He is the true God. Rahab said, "[F]or the Lord your God is he who is God in heaven above and on earth beneath" (Josh. 2:11).
   b. She makes the spies promise to save her and her family. The spies tell her to tie a red cord in the window, and that house and everything in it would be preserved.
   c. Her virtues are wisdom, courage, and faith, to name a few.

8. A:

   a. Rahab, once she believed, acted upon her belief.
   b. The Kingdom of God is open to all who believe. Rahab was a woman of questionable occupation, but her actions were those of faith. Jesus was a descendent, then, of both Jews and Gentiles, of the holy and the disreputable. Why? Jesus came to save the lost of both Israel and the nations.

Lesson 4
Deborah and Jael, Ruth and Hannah: Women of the Judges

Prelude
1. A:
    a. The problem with doing whatever we feel like, or moredeceptively, what "our heart is telling us," is that we are fallen beings, and our feelings will, at times (if not often), lead us to do what is contrary to God's law of love and selflessness. The fact of the matter is that there is absolute truth. Just because a person feels that it is okay to get drunk or contracept or abort her baby does not make these actions right or good. These are evils whether we feel they are wrong or not. It is the same old deception of the Devil, and the same old sin of Adam and Eve—God must be withholding something good (we think), and out of our mistaken pride, we feel it is okay to do what we want.

    b. The consequences in popular culture are the same as they were in ancient culture: the emotional, physical, spiritual, and intellectual slaying of humanity. Both then and now, we see rampant divorce, abortion, contraception, homosexual activity, drug abuse, immodesty, sexual promiscuity, and a general acceptance of what is evil as good.

Deborah and Jael
2. A:
    a. Deborah agrees to go, but warns Barak that this militaryvictory will not make him a hero because God will deliver Sisera into the hand of a woman.

    b. Jael, when given the opportunity, brought Sisera into her tent, and while he was sleeping, she stuck a tent peg through his skull.

3. A:

  a. Deborah was a leader and a motivator full of faith and courage. She believed that God was with the Hebrews and would accomplish great things for them.

  b. All of Deborah's virtues are worthy of emulation. Many situations call for these virtues. Getting your family to pray the Rosary, organizing a parish activity, and even organizing a group to do this Bible study are situations in which the virtues of Deborah are needed and could be practiced.

4. A: Jael prefigures the fulfillment of the prophesy concerning Mary and the crushing of the serpent's head (cf. Gen. 3:15). Jael crushes the head of the enemy of Israel, while Mary will crush the head of the Enemy of all the children of God. Deborah the prophetess calls Jael "blessed of women" and Elizabeth, the mother of the last Old Covenant prophet, addresses Mary, "Blessed are you among women" (Judg. 5:24; Lk. 1:42).

Ruth

5. A: Ruth was loyal, courageous, humble, a hard worker, and docile.

6. Allow the women to share their responses.

7. A: Ruth was a good woman, who, through love and devotion, left her home to come to Israel. She is a good example of a Gentile who leaves what is comfortable in order to cling to what is true and beloved. Also, the Moabites were enemies of Israel, and so by including Ruth in the genealogy of Jesus, Saint Matthew is listing not only another Gentile, but also an enemy. The inclusion of women in Jesus' genealogy emphasizes God's desire to save all people.

Hannah

8. A: Hannah desires to have a child to offer to the Lord.

9. A: Hannah believed that her child came from the Lord and that God is all powerful. Allow the women to share their answers.

10. A: A religious vocation is a special grace. As Hannah shows us, our children are given us by God, and we should offer them back to Him with gladness if they are called to serve in this way.

Lesson 5
Abigail, Michal, and Bathsheba: Women of the Kings

Abigail

1. A: David had prevented the plundering of Nabal's shepherds and sheep in Carmel. David's men came to him on a feast day in need of food, and Nabal rudely turned them away.

2. A: The servant told Abigail about the problem because Abigail was "of good understanding" and because he knew she would do what was necessary to preserve the household (1 Sam. 25:3).

3. A: She was industrious and prudent.

4. A: Imitating Abigail's quick thinking and discretion can help lead us to true prosperity.

Michal

5. A:

   a.–d. Allow the women to share their responses. You can encourage them to use the chart in Appendix II to plot their growth in virtue.

   I: Vanity is a sin of misplaced priorities and distorted love of self. One strategy for overcoming the vice of vanity is growing in our love of God. Prayer and reading the Gospels can help us do so.

   A:
   e. She was unable to have children.
   f. Barrenness was a sign of disgrace among Hebrew women. Her barrenness would have acutely affected her sense of vanity.

Bathsheba

6. A:

a. David's sin with Bathsheba was one of the greatest sins of his life. God did not forget that Bathsheba was made David's wife by illicit means, and so Saint Matthew listed her as the wife of Uriah.

b. Adultery is a sin against the covenant of marriage. It is a sin that aims at the destruction of the fabric of a marriage: trust, solidarity, selflessness, and the sacredness of the marriage bed. It is also a sin against the rights of one's spouse (cf. Catechism, no 2380-81.)

c. One practical habit is avoiding intimate, opposite sex friendships—who knows when the friendship will turn into something more? Other habits include avoiding intimate conversations with members of the opposite sex and limiting time alone with them. If you find yourself attracted to someone other than your spouse, flee the situation or context of your relationship with that person.

7. A: David probably felt he owed a debt to Bathsheba. Solomon was the firstborn of their marriage and was also the first son born to them after the death of their son from the adulterous affair.

8.

a.–b. Allow the women to share their ideas.

9. A:

a. He bowed to her and had a seat for her at his right hand—the seat of powerful influence. He said he would grant any of her requests.

b. Mary is the Queen Mother who intercedes on our behalf, and the King will not refuse her. Unlike Bathsheba, she will not request anything that would hurt the King.

Lesson 6
Esther, Judith, and the Maccabean Mother:
Women of the Exile and Return

Judith
1. A:
    a. She wore sackcloth and the clothes of a widow, and she also fasted frequently.

    b. She was treated with respect because she feared God and had great devotion to Him.

    c. She was renowned for her wisdom, which was attributed to her pure heart. Similarly, God gave Solomon wisdom because of his own pure desires.

2. A:
    a. She first admonished them for testing God and imposing time limits upon His plans. She then told them that they needed to pray.

    b. She said that their present situation was a test of their faithfulness.

3. A: Judith prayed, "[C]rush their arrogance by the hand of a woman" (Jud. 9:10). Deborah likewise prophesied that the enemy would be given "into the hand of a woman" (Judg. 4:9).

4. A: While Judith lied to Holofernes about what the Israelites would do, she was truthful about the laws of God, about herself, and about her intention to keep regular prayers.

5. A:
    a. When he had passed out because of all the wine he had drunk, she cut off his head with his own sword and had her maid put it in her food bag.

    b. They are both proclaimed blessed among women. Judith, like Jael, is a type of Mary. As Judith crushed the head of the enemy, Mary crushes the head of the serpent.

6. A: Her reputation for godliness, as well as God's favor upon her and her people, protected them from their enemies.

Esther
7. a.–c. Allow the women to share their thoughts.

8. A:
   a. Allow the women to share their responses.
   b. Praying at regular times every day is one way to establish the habit of prayer. Allow the women to share their own ideas.

9. A:
   a. Allow the women to share their own ideas. The unborn, children, and the elderly are all in need of defense, and those who are defenseless need a voice.
   b. Brainstorm as a group about what you could do. Think of practical ways you and other parishioners can help those in need.

The Maccabean Mother
10. A:
   a. God was the source of her faith.
   b. She hoped in God's power and in an eternal reward from Him.
   c. She loved her sons and the Lord.

11. a–b. Allow the women to share their thoughts.

12. a–b. Allow the women to share their thoughts and ideas.

13. a–b. Allow the women to share their thoughts and ideas.
   c. A faithful friend or spiritual director could help keep you accountable to your commitments.

Lesson 7
Mary Magdalene: Woman of the Ministry

1. A: Mary was among the small group of Jesus' disciples who traveled with the apostles and provided for them.

2. Allow the women to share their answers. Christ has healed all of us of original sin, and as we grow in the spiritual life, we can see how areas of personal sin in our lives begin to diminish. In this way, Christ is healing us.

3. A:
    a. Her love for Jesus motivated her.
    b. She must have been full of courage, faith, hope, and love.
    c.–e. Allow the women the opportunity to share their ideas.

4. A:
    a. Mary was devoted to Jesus. She loved Him and her actions showed it. She was willing to risk her life by being present at the Crucifixion, and she overcame her exhaustion to go to the tomb.
    b. Allow the women to share their responses.

5. A:
    a. She remained at the tomb, weeping. When she saw someone she thought was a gardener, she begged him for the body of Jesus.
    b. She was the first person mentioned in Scripture as seeing the Risen Christ and became the apostle to the apostles.
    c. God rewards love and devotion with the grace to understand His truth and to see His love even more clearly.

6. A:

    a. Jesus came to redeem all of humanity. He knew that the Fall caused division and discord, disrespect and abuse. Jesus chose to allow women to play an integral part in His own life because we are an integral part of humanity.

    b. All of these events were milestones in Jesus' ministry, and at each event, women participated as servants and helpers.

    c. Allow the women to share their ideas.

Lesson 8
Mary: Mother of God and His Church

1. A:

   a. Mary kept quiet and "considered in her mind what sort of greeting this might be" (Lk. 1:29). She believed the angel, and then she asked a question so that she could understand God's plan more deeply.

   b. Unlike Mary, Zechariah doubted the angel at first and responded to the angel with a question based on his doubt.

   c. Like Mary, we should reflect quietly and pray before we speak or act.

2. A: Mary asked her question because she had made a vow to God. If she had not made a vow of virginity, she would have had no need to ask how she would become a mother. She was not making excuses or questioning the power of God, as did Zechariah; rather, she was concerned about fulfilling her vows. Gabriel's response confirms her vow.

3. A:

   a. God wanted Mary to become the Mother of God the Son.

   b. Allow the women to share their thoughts.

4. A:

   a. Mary, newly pregnant, "went with haste" to serve hercousin Elizabeth (Lk. 1:39). In not wasting time, but rather going to help her cousin, Mary showed her charity and industriousness.

   b. He leapt for joy.

5. A:

   a. She refers to herself as lowly and a servant while referring to God as mighty and holy. She had a proper perspective

on her relationship to God: She knew she was a creature
before the Creator.
b. Yes.

6. A:
a. Mary reflected quietly upon her life and that of her Son.
b. We should reflect quietly before we speak or act.

7. A:
a. She may have been serving at the wedding. In any
case,she had a great love and concern for the couple that
made her attentive to them and their needs.
b. She knew that He had the power to do something
aboutthe problem and that it would be a disgrace to the
couple if they ran out of wine. Mary was sensitive to their
needs and feelings.
c. "Do whatever he tells you" (Jn. 2:5).

8. A:
a. God has made her our spiritual Mother, and she intercedes
for us at the right hand of God as the Queen Mother of
Heaven and Earth.
b. Our devotion to her should manifest itself in
prayers,respect, and honor.

9. A: She devoted herself to prayer with the apostles and other
followers of Jesus.

10. A: Allow the women to share their thoughts. Mary is an
icon of the Church, and her Assumption is a symbol of our
eternal destiny.

11. a.–c. Allow the women to share their responses and
thoughts.

MORE BIBLE STUDIES FOR WOMEN!

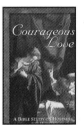

Courageous Love:
A Bible Study on Holiness for Women
by Stacy Mitch / **$9.95**, 113 pages
Courageous Love examines the teaching of Sacred Scripture on women and the feminine pursuit of holiness.

Courageous Virtue:
A Bible Study on Moral Excellence for Women
by Stacy Mitch / **$9.95**, 102 pages
A treasure chest of wisdom, *Courageous Virtue* offers practical ways to grow in the moral virtues and in faith, hope, and love.

Woman of Grace:
A Bible Study for Married Women
by Michaelann Martin / **$11.95**, 149 pages
Woman of Grace is an insightful and intimate Bible study written to help married women grow in holiness in their day-to-day living. Michaelann Martin offers guidance to women who seek to deepen their prayer lives and find fulfillment in their vocation as wives and mothers.

(800) 398-5470
www.emmausroad.org

EMMAUS ROAD
PUBLISHING